T0065416

THE AMERICAN
★ DREAM ★

Where You Start Doesn't Determine
Where You Finish

Carson Steen

authorHOUSE®

AuthorHouse™
1663 Liberty Drive
Bloomington, IN 47403
www.authorhouse.com
Phone: 833-262-8899

Published by AuthorHouse 11/10/2020

ISBN: 978-1-6655-0732-5 (sc)
ISBN: 978-1-6655-0730-1 (hc)
ISBN: 978-1-6655-0731-8 (e)

Library of Congress Control Number: 2020922250

Print information available on the last page.

Cover picture - Carson Steen built this replica model of the old home place he grew up at.

This book is printed on acid-free paper.

This book is dedicated to the following:

My mother Gracie Mae Steen Anderson, who died when I was just six weeks old.

My great uncle and great aunt Mack and Lara Steen, who raised me from six weeks old to a young man.

My late wife Kathleen King Steen, sons Ricky and Robby Steen and all my grandchildren to whom I'm very proud of.

GOD, who gave me the ability to write this book.

How growing up in the 1940's and 50's helped me realize I had to respect others for them to have respect for me.

Gracie Mae Steen Anderson   Carson Donald Steen

The autobiography of Carson Donald Steen
Born in Chesterfield County South Carolina to
Wade Atwood Anderson and Gracie Mae Steen
Anderson on the 5th day February 1940

My great grandfather John C. Steen and his wife
Polly Miles Steen holding their daughter Nettie

Sam Steen

My great grandfather on my grandmother's side of the family

———————————— ★ ————————————

I was born at home in a four-room house about ¼ mile from the house I grew up in.

My mother, Gracie May Steen Anderson died when I was six weeks old from infection after child birth. My father Wade Haywood Anderson deeded me to my great uncle Maxie Robert Steen, a world war one veteran that had never been marred and lived with his father John C. Steen and Sister Lara Jane Steen who also had never been marred. They gave me as much love as any biological parents could have ever given me. Most people have never heard of a deed of a child, but it was a practice used up to the 1940's until it was stopped in the late 40's. I have a copy of the deed that's recorded in the Chesterfield County court house. It plainly states the deed of a child, and states that the person the child was deeded to agreed to support the child as it was his biological child, and had full control and responsibility of the child until the child was 21 years of age.

I grew up in an old house on a small farm, the older part of the house was built with logs, and at some time later siding had been put over the logs. Where some of the siding had come loose you could see the logs that were tied together with wooden pegs, there were no electricity or running water in the house, it had wooden windows shutters, and there were no screens over the windows or no screen doors. In the spring and summer flies and insects were so terrible you had to continue fighting them inside the house to be able to eat your dinner. We heated in the winter with wood in a fire place, and our toilets were outside. Our food was cooked on a wood stove and we got our water from an outside well that was equipped with a chain, tackle, and bucket. The water was drown by hand and brought inside in a water bucket, and we used a dipper to get water out of the bucket when we needed it.

In the winter when it got below freezing and you drew water from the well the chain would have ice on it where it had got wet. In the house we would have to break the dipper lose from ice in the bucket after it set overnight to get water. The bedroom would get below freezing on a cold night as well.

We would have so much cover on the bed in the winter to keep warm, it was hard to turn over, there were no insulation in the house walls or ceilings, and when you got warm you didn't won't to get up, but with all the chores you had to do, you had to get up early to take care of the animals and the chores we had to do each day. We would get up in the morning and go through a breeze way to the kitchen which was another part of the house where the kitchen was with a fire place and a wood burning stove, but the fire being burned out from the night before, you had to restart it with the temperature below freezing. With enough clothes on to keep warm you would go to the barn, feed and water the animals and return to the house, by this time, if you were lucky, the fire would be burning good enough you could get warm. Then the wood stove would need to be fired up to cook breakfast, this was an ongoing thing each morning. Today we have central air, heat and insulation throughout our houses. We seem to forget what the good old days were like, if they could be called good old days. This didn't mean that we were worse off than other people, most people in that time lived the same way in the country. It was the way of life.

Our only source for light at night back then was kerosene lamps. We would have to go through the breeze way from the kitchen to the main part of the house where the bed rooms was, carrying a lamp that would blow out if a small puff of wind happened to blow by, then you would be in the dark for the rest of the way. We would always blow the lamp out when we went to bed it was never left burning due to safety risk.

We had no radio or television in those days, our only entertainment was at night when neighbors would visit or we would visit them to talk and tell stories about experiences of the past. We would almost always have visitors at night or we would visit our friends and talk until around eleven o'clock and go home and get ready for bed. This was what we always looked forward to. People in those days seemed to be much closer to each other, I guess it was because we had to depend on each other more than we do today and we had respect for each other.

I remember my aunt would put news paper on the walls in our bed rooms. The bed room was large and had three beds, she would use news paper and a paste made with flower and water that she mixed together until it got to the right thickness, and used a brushed to put it on the walls, and would place the news paper over the pasted walls and smooth it out and let it dry, and after it dried it would stay in place from then on. It not only looked good after being installed, but would help light up the room with the white paper, and help keep the cold air out in the winter where it would come in through small cracks in the walls. You would do whatever you could to help keep the heat inside. I can tell younger people today about what we went through back then, and they will look at me like they think I'm losing my mind, they can't understand what it was like because they haven't had to go through anything like it. You could also lie in the bed at night and read the news papers on the wall until you blew the lamp out and went to sleep.

Back in the 40's and 50's we had a Watkens dealer that would come by about once a month. He would drive a car with the back seat removed and a shelve built in its place where he would carry his products with the Watkens brand name on them. He had everything from cold medication to floor mops and ever thing in between. He would give you a catalog so you could look through it and see what he had and be ready to buy it the next time he come through. There were also a Raleigh Product dealer that would come by usually between the times of the Watkens dealers visit; he had about the same products except they had the Raleigh Products name on them.

There were a lot of people traveling the country selling deferent things in those days, they were people selling rugs and other selling candy, and trying to get their customers to sell candy for them, work was hard to find back then and everybody was looking for ways to make a living for their family and they sold a lot of products for it would keep people from having to go to a store, and would save a lot of time when they needed to be working.

I remember listening to stories about world war one where my uncle had fought in Germany, and some of the things he had to go through. He told about having to go to war and how he caught a train to New Port News VA and how they boarded a ship to go overseas, he told how the ship was on the water for several days going overseas to France, and how they had to watch for mines that had been put in their path by the enemy to blow the ships up, and how you could hear a mine scraping the side of the ship, and expecting it to explode at any minute, torpedoes being fired from enemy submarines and how you could see them with binoculars coming toward your ship, just under the water and how the Captain would try and change course to dodge the torpedo's.

He said when they got to France, how they had to walk and carrying all their equipment, because back then there was vary a few vehicles, and how horses would pull wagons to help carry supplies, and cannons mounted on two wheel carts, and how they would have to dig trenches on the front lines to keep low enough so the enemy fire would go over their head, I remember him telling about one of his comrades talking to him in a trench when they were receiving enemy fire, and his comrade said I wish they would quit this craziness and let us go home, just as he finished talking a snipers bullet hit him in the head between his eyes, my uncle said he didn't even make a noise when he was hit, just stopped talking. Another time he told about looking across a field on the front line and could see the broom sage shaking from being hit by machine gun bullets. And would tell how his platoon had broken the Hindenburg line before the war ended. Back then I had no other kids to play with so I would set and listen to their stories. I couldn't imagine how bad it was. The war had to be a terrible thing to live through.

When I was very young I remember seeing a group of cattle being drove down a road close to our house, you could see them for about a quarter mile as they were drove by with two people on horses back past our house keeping them on the road, I remember they had long horns and were making a mooing noise as they walked all bunched together, I was told they were being drove to a cattle sale to be sold. What was so unusual I had seen pictures in books of cattle drives in the west, but never in the south east where we lived. The two men on the horses would ride on each side of the road and keep the cattle moving in a group. If some got out of the group the horsemen would drive them back in the pack and keep them moving. For a young child this was amazing to watch.

I remember being told about my great great grandfather F. P. Steen who fought in the War Between the States and how he had to travel many miles to other parts of the country and would be gone for a long period of time without his family hearing from him or knowing whether he was dead or alive. Back then there was not much way for the solders to get word back home to their families except by mail, and during the war it wasn't always a sure thing that the mail would get through. So their families didn't know whether they were dead or alive. They would travel on horseback not knowing when they would come in contact with the enemy, and sleep where ever they happened to be or whatever the weather was with someone always standing guard.

Back home I was told the Union soldiers from the North would invade our part of the country, riding through the neighborhoods on their horses and take anything they wanted, I was told they would catch chickens off the yard and tie their feet together and throw them across their horses backs and ride off, and they would destroy all that was left behind, People that had any money, I was told would bury it when they heard the Union solders was coming, They were several pots and jars with money buried and after the war they couldn't remember where they buried it or they had died without telling anybody where it was buried. I was told if anybody resisted they would be shot on the spot. The women and young girls would be raped and molested. They were described as a bunch rowdy men doing whatever they wanted to do and nobody could do anything about it. It must have been pure hell.

There was some money found and dug up after I was born in 1940 that were buried during the civil war that I can remember people talking about, some people would bury the money and forget where they buried it. There was a road through our property called the Tory Road that was said to be the road the Union Solders traveled when they were passing through our neighborhood, I remember playing in the old road beds when I was small and you could see where the road was, and parts of it were still being traveled. This must have been pure hell during the war here in your own back yard.

I have a medal that was found that belonged to my great great grandfather who fought in the civil war, with his name on a bar above the medal, he was dead long before I was born but I heard many stores about him and the civil war from his son, my great grandfather who passed away when I was about twelve years old. This had to be one of the worst times for our country. This medal was found near Fort mill SC by a man that worked with me, and by the last name on the medal being the same as mine he asked me if I knew a F. P. Steen. And I told him my great great grandfather was F. P. Steen and served in the Civil War, he then told me about this medal and how his son found it at an old house place on the Brick Yard road on the outskirts of Fort Mill, and he thought I should have it. After he gave it to me, I told a reporter at the Fort Mill Times about it, and he wanted to write an article about it that was written in the Fort Mill

Times about the medal being found and all the descriptions on it. I have no idea how the medal got to this area of the country.

I have several original deeds where my great great grandfather bought land at prices under two dollars per acre in the late 1800's and I still own some of that land now. It is amazing to me how people lived in those days and what they had to go through. Most people really don't realize how good we have it today. Another thing I remember about our farm were the ditches that was dug about three foot wide and about three foot deep through the fields, I was told they were to drain the water away from the crops when we got a lot of rain, these ditches were laid out in a manner to drain the water according to the lay of the land. Although our land was sandy it was low enough to hold water. Over all of our property there was at least two miles of ditches dug by hand long before I was born and all small trees had to be cut out and removed every year or two to keep the ditches open. I remember seeing water running through these ditches after a rain. I have some old deeds where this land was sold for one dollar and fifty cents per acre. Most people today don't believe these prices paid for land, but I have old deeds to prove it.

As I was growing up I remember playing in one of the wooded areas of our property and remember a saw dust pile in part of the wooded area, I was always told not to go around the saw dust pile because it had been on fire for several years and could cave in. I remember seeing smoke coming out of the top several times. The pile was probably 20 feet tall or taller and 30 to 40 feet across, the saw dust pile was surly a lot bigger before it started burning and decaying. The saw mill was there long before I was born and probably was used to cut lumber to build all the building that was built on the property including the house. There were several building including barns and sheds with horse or mule stalls, this was all built before I was born. The saw mill had to have been there a long time ago because trees had grown to full size around the saw dust pile. I often wonder what it was like to live in those days, being told what it was like is not like living it. It would have been good to have known my ancestors that I was told about.

There was a clay pit in the edge of a field which was unusual in this part of the country. I was told that the county got clay from the pit to build roads many years earlier, and left it open. After it rained I would play in the clay pit and get red clay on my clothe and my aunt would get upset about it being so hard to get out and threaten me if I got in that clay pit anymore. There were two muscadine vines at the edge of the pit, one white verity and one black where we always got muscadines when they got ripe in late summer.

There was not much for a child to do in those days for entertainment except ramble in the woods and look at nature and unusual things we could find, there were no electronics or radio or television, it was mostly bare nature, and I think I learned a lot because my mind wasn't being occupied by fiction like kids are occupied with today. That might be why I can remember a lot of details about what was happening around me as I was growing up. I was always told to listen to elders because I could learn a lot about life by paying attention to what was being said and was told to stay alert of things around me, and when elders was talking to listen not talk.

When I was about six years old a man come to our house, I remember he drove a fairly new black car, I assume he was the county engineer, he talked to my uncle about buying sand clay off the property to put a top on the sandy roads to help the base become harder. When they agreed on the price, a crew of men was sent out to test a piece of land that we grew corn on. They used a large drill to take samples of the dirt to make sure it was suitable for what they were going use it for, they found it was what they wanted and started removing the top soil to get down to the sand clay. The dirt they removed was carried down the hill and spread across a low place in the road where they were going to haul the dirt across. This was in the summer and was dry at the time. Not knowing how much water would come down this branch when it rained, they built the road up about four foot high with no drain pipe. They hauled several loads of dirt across this road, which become a dam and packed the dirt down until it was hard. After they got all the sand clay they needed and moved all their equipment out it started to rain, as it rained it started filling up until it reached the top and started running around the end of the dam. This is the way I saw everything happened through a child's eyes because I was very young at the time.

The dam continued to hold water and after a few years we found that we had fish in the pond and didn't know how they got there. Over the next several years we would fish in the pond and catch a lot of fish. When I left to move to Fort Mill in 1959 the pond was still there and I assume it still had a lot of fish.

Most of our farm land was sandy and soft with very little clay, and was rich with black dirt, it would grow anything but we always used plenty of fertilizer to help the dirt stay rich. My uncle once told me that you could only use ground so much without putting the fertilizer back in or it would get where it would not grow anything as well as it should. I was taught to always take care of whatever you used so it would take care of you in the future, and the land was no different. It is hard for me to get out of the ways I was brought up, and that is why I still work a garden every year and get a great satisfaction out of watching it grow and giving what we don't use to our friends.

What I learned growing up is some of the most important lessons I ever learned, I was told to always treat all people like I would like to be treated and I could go to sleep at night know I hadn't mistreated anyone and feel good about the way I was living my life, and to work hard and not be lazy and God would help me to become a man that would be respected and always have friends when I needed them. Over the years I've found that to be true. And those words have remained with me all my life and will until the day I die. I know I have done a lot of things throughout my life that I'm not proud of, but I always ask God to forgive me and help me to learn by my mistakes and not make them again.

I remember when my uncle rented part of our farm to a young black man and his family to farm, and was talking to him about how to get the best yields out of his crop and told him to always use plenty of fertilizer and it would pay off in the fall and the next year. This man always had a great yield each year and always used plenty of fertilizer as my uncle instructed him to do. He was one of the hardest working young man I had ever seen and would listen to advice from anyone that could help him. At that time he had two young children and it was hard to make enough money to take care of his family, but he would do anything he had to do to support them. As I grew up I always thought of them as part of my family. He was the most dedicated man to his family and friends I ever knew.

When I was about five years old I remember we had a smoke house where we would keep our meat hanging after it was cured in white sacks, it was usually hanging throughout the ceiling in the smokehouse and there were tables on both sides to stack meat on while it was curing. I remember I would sneak a knife out of the kitchen, go in the smoke house and cut a small hole in the sack and cut a piece of meat off a ham and eat it there. It wasn't because I was hungry but it was different, we always had plenty of food to eat, but I thought the cured meat was better before being cooked. Although this meat was raw it never hurt me. One day I was caught in the smoke house getting some raw meat and was told by my aunt to never eat meat without it being cooked because it could make me sick, but for some reason it never tasted the same after it was cooked, and the raw meat never made me sick.

We always had our hogs that we grew in the spring and summer for butchering in early winter, in a wire fence with a shed to keep the rain out, and pine straw for their beds, we would feed them inside the wire fence in a hog trough located away from the shed to help keep their bed from getting routed up and to keep it dry. Hogs can be very messy. We would always have 6 to 8 hogs and pigs at all times and one or two males for breeding. I can remember the female hogs called Sows, having as many as 10 piglets, we would grow them out during the spring and summer and get ready to butcher when it got cold enough to help the meat cure, in the environment we lived in the weather was never cool except in the winter to keep the meat from spoiling, there were no refrigeration in those days to keep a storage area cool enough to cure the meat.

We always salt cured our meat and hung it in the smoke house in sacks when it took salt and we also put a lot of black pepper on it to help it cure better and keep the insects away. My uncle was always the one who salted the meat for curing, and was good at it, never losing any meat due to spoilage. He put the meat on a clean white sheet with the skin down and spread salt over it about a 1/8 inch thick. He would use his hands to rub it in, he spent a lot of time rubbing the meat and adding more salt until he got it like he wanted, as he rubbed the meat it would get warm and the salt would melt and go in, He would then turn it over with the skin up and let it set covered on a table with black pepper and salt and let it set for several days. He said it needed to soak in with the skin down and after several days turn the skin up to let the moister drain out. After the meat took salt and started to cure he would put it in white cloth sacks and hang it in the smoke house. There's nothing better than salt cured ham on hot biscuits in the morning with a cup of coffee.

We always had a flock of chickens running around the house, about 25 or 30 with usually about three roosters, we would use the eggs, except the ones the hens set on to hatch more chicks. The hens would hide their nest with sometime 12 to 15 eggs in them and would set on the nest until the chicks hatched, When they were hatched they would come off the nest and follow the hen everywhere she went and if anybody or thing got close to them she would flog them to protect her baby chicks. We always butchered and cooked the roosters that were hatched after they got grew up, except we always would keep three to bread the hens. And as the hens got older we would thin the oldest out, which were the ones we used for food.

I would always play under the house, which set on block pillows about two and a half foot high and was open with no underpinning, the chickens always roamed under the house and I would play with the little chicks, some time one of the hens with the small chicks would flog me but they had no spurs and couldn't hurt, but we had a big red rooster that were aggressive and would always spur the dogs, they would holler and run away. His spurs were about one inch long and had a sharp end.

One day I was playing under the house when the rooster come up to my side and all of a sudden hit me on the side of my head behind my ear and his spur cut me behind my left ear and the blood started running down my neck and on my shirt, I ran out and when I got in the house my aunt asked what happened and I said the red rooster spurred me, she cleaned up the spot he spurred and got it to stop bleeding and said I'll take care of him, the following Sunday we had chicken and dumplings for dinner.

When I was small, I remember there was a black folk's church on top of a hill; the church was called Nicey Grove, about a quarter mile from our house. When they would have a revival in the summer they would have all the church windows open because there were no air condition in those days, We would set on our porch and listen to some of the best Gospel singing I have ever heard, we could hear them as good as if we were in there church, and we could also hear the preacher, and they didn't have PA Systems back then, they just really got into praising the Lord and the sound would travel a long way at night when it was quite outside. It was always a blessing to set on the porch and listen to their singing and preaching, sometimes they would preach and sing until after midnight. That is memories I will never forget.

When I was about five or six years old about once a month the county would scrape the roads by our house, it always amazed me to watch. They used a Caterpillar to pull an iron wheel road grader with a chain gang prisoner standing on a platform on the back of the grader to keep the blade in the right position using two hand wheels.

They would scrape a dome shape on the road to help the water run to the ditches and then would pull the dirt out of the ditches and spread it to the outside edge of fields. They always took pride in the way they would leave the roads, that's the way people worked back then. The Caterpillar driver was always a county employee who would never leave the job until it was like he though it should be.

After the roads were scraped the chain gang with ten or fifteen prisoners wearing striped pants and shirts would clean out road tiles and cut bushes on the side of the road. The guard who watched them, his name was Josh Brooks, carried a double barreled shot gun and would walk along the road while they worked. Some prisoners would have chains on their legs if they had tried to run away in the past.

Some would have to drag a large steel ball along as they worked. If a person ever had to go to the chain gang once they wouldn't won't to go back again.

At twelve o'clock the prisoners would be fed lunch along the road where ever they happened to be. They each would get a steel bowel and a jar of water with a spoon to eat with, there bowls would be filled with pinto beans and they would be given a piece of corn bread, they had thirty minutes to eat, and went back to work. They weren't allowed to talk to anyone while they were working or when they were eating except when the guard would talk to them. No one wanted to go to the chain gang back then, that's why we didn't need locks on our doors.

I remember my uncle Mack had a Bible on a shelf close where he set by the fire place at night. He was never big on going to church but he would put on his glasses, take his seat by the fire place and read the Bible, and could talk about what he read if anybody would ask. I still have that Bible today. He and my aunt or great grandfather who was paralyzed in his side didn't go to church very much but were well aware of the importance of keeping Gods commandments and would talk about them and always told me how important Gods word was, they also talked to me about doing what was right in Gods eyes and always have respect for His word. And never take anything that didn't belong to me. I know without any doubt that God has been with me thought-out my life, even times when I didn't deserve it, but I'm grateful. I have never been the type of guy to preach to others about their religion but always tried to teach my children to live the kind of life that God would want them to and always witness about what He has done for me, but I believe everybody have to make their own choice, but need to hear about God and know he is there for you if you believe in him. Thank God both of our sons have respect for others and go to church on Sundays along with their children.

Another time I remember I got very sick and stayed that way for several days. And back then in the mid 1940's doctors would make house calls, my uncle Mack some way got in touch with doctor Griggs, the doctor that delivered me when I was born, and asked if he could come by, and take a look at me while he was visiting another patient in our neighborhood, he stopped by, checked me and looked in my throat and told my uncle that I had deapthurea, and I needed a shot, that he could give me, so he proceeded to get a needle with medicine in a glass tube that the needle was attached to. The needle looked like it was five inches long, and said I would have to get the shot in my stomach. I was scared to death as he stuck that needle in my navel and it hurt so bad I thought I was going to die, when he got through he told my uncle if I weren't better In about three days to bring me to his office. After the three days I felt a little better but I told my uncle I felt good, I didn't want to get another shot in my stomach. I finely got better, but I never wanted another shot like that, I was told later that they had to give the shot in the stomach that was the only way the shot would be successful. I guess that's why I don't like needles to this day.

When I was about seven or eight years old I got one of my uncles Mack's twelve ga. Shot gun shells that he always kelp in a dresser drawer in his bed room, I wanted to know what made them shoot, so cut it open removed the shot and the powder and proceeded to pry the cap out of the brass part of the end of the shell, it was hard to get out but I succeeded to remove it, I thought after I removed the powder and shot from the case it would be safe, this cap is so small it can't be dangers, so I laid it on an anvil in the back yard and hit it with a hammer, it made a loud noise and knocked the hammer out of my hand, and I couldn't hear a thing for several minutes, my aunt come out the door asking what was that noise, I said I couldn't hear a thing. I didn't play with gun shells any more. And please never leave ammunition where a child can get their hands on it because they don't realize the dangers.

Some of my school friends and I would get together and play baseball on the sandy dirt road in front of our house, you could see a car coming a quarter mile down the road, there was very little traffic on the roads back then and we could play in the roads fairly safe, I was the back catcher behind the batter, and would keep getting closer and closer when the batter swung to hit the ball I finely got too close behind him and the bat hit me over my right eye, that's when the lights went out, when I come too they were people all around me and, I was very dizzy and when I felt of my head there was a knot above my eye the size of an egg, everybody was scared and shaking me and was upset, I finely told them I was ok and went to the house where my aunt put a cold cloth on my head. The knot finely went down but I had a headache for several days. I never played back catcher anymore. I was always wanting to know what made things work. After going several years without a vehicle my uncle Mack bought a 1938 chevolate pickup. It had been owned by a Mr. Blakeley in Pageland SC who had a heart attack while driving and hit a tree damaging the left front fender. He bought it from his wife and brought it home, repaired the front fender and used it for several years. When the motor bearings started making a noise, he made a pair of wood ramps in the yard out of large boards, drove it on the ramps to get to the bottom pan where he could remove it to get to the bearings, I was really excited about being able to see inside the motor. And when he removed the oil pan I was always laying on the ground watching every move he made and asked as many questions as I could think of. I watched him remove a connecting rod cap them put it in an old farm vice that were mounted on a post in the yard, He used a file to remove some metal so the bearing would fit tighter around the crankshaft journal, and replaced it. After all six were done and the oil pan replaced he put new oil in and filled it to the proper level and it ran great.

The most important thing in my life was when at about six years old, I was playing on the back porch, the wind had been blowing that night and blown a shingle off the top of the house, the shingle had a nail that was just right to stick in my foot when I stepped on it. I was barefoot and felt it penetrate deep in the ball of my foot and the pain was real bad, I tried to pull it out but it hurt so bad when I pulled on it I could not stand the pain, I set down on the floor looked at it and wondered what I was going to do, when I remembered what I had been told that God would always help you if you asked, So I asked God to help me get the nail out, moments later to my surprise the nail fell out of my foot with no pain and hit the floor, I couldn't believe what I was seeing, but it happened. From that moment on my faith in God have been strong knowing He was always with me, and protected me even when I strayed away and did things I knew were wrong, and from that day on I've always thanked Him for taking care of me, My faith has always been strong and the most important thing in my life.

I was always pulling tricks on somebody. One of my uncles who were about a year older than me had been shooting small fire crackers that day and we had some left. My great grandfather, John was in his late sixtes, had had a stroke and was paralyzed on his right side, and walked with a walking stick, he would always set in a chair by the side of the fireplace. He would smoke a crocked stem pipe and when he finisher he would knock the ashes out and refill the pipe with tobacco, pack it down and set it on the winder sill for the next time. It was close to Christmas and I had some of these real small fire crackers left over, they were called penny firecrackers. I decided to have some fun, and when he went to bed I sneaked over, got his pipe, took all the tobacco out and placed a firecracker in the bowl of the pipe, wound the fuse up neatly and refilled the pipe with tobacco packed it back down and placed it back in the same place. He was always late getting up in the morning and I had found a crack in the outside wall that I could see through. The next morning I was peeking through the crack when he come in and set down in his chair, reached over and got his pipe and a strike anywhere match he had in a box and lit it, he took a couple of big draws and nothing happened, he took another draw or two when all of a sudden the pipe exploded, and he was left with only the pipes crocked stem hanging in his mouth, that's when I started laughing and got scared and ran to the barn where he couldn't see me, he never saw me and I never saw his reaction after the explosion, and he never talked about it to anyone afterwards. But I'll never forget that pipe coming apart and going in all directions and him holding the stem in his mouth wondering what had happened. I did some dumb things as a kid, but it was funny and he didn't get hurt. I would never think of doing anything like that today to anybody.

I remember watching my uncle trim the huffs on the mule's feet when they would grow too long, he would do this about once a year, I was always asking questions about why he was cutting there huffs, and did it hurt them when he cut them, he said it didn't hurt them and, he said if you didn't keep them trimmed it would hurt them when they walked. You had to take care of the mules that helped you make a living and if they were not healthy you could not expect them to work all day and pull a plow. If the huffs were not trimmed they would split and break off and cause the animal to favor that foot because it hurt when they walked. He would hold the mules foot up between his legs and cut the huff all the way around with a tool that would bite a piece of huff off and used a rasp to smooth it out and then check to see how well it fit on a board which would represent the ground, if it wasn't right he would work on it again until he got all four feet even, when the mule would move around you could tell they could walk better, He never used horse shoes on the mules because he said if you would keep the huffs trimmed properly the mule could walk better and feel naturally.

My uncle Mack would take his pickup truck to the fields when we were pulling fodder to feed the mules in the winter. We always planted a few watermelons between the corn, so when we were working in the corn field in the fall we could find a watermelon to cut or burst and eat which was always a treat, when he parked the pickup in the field I would sneak around and find a watermelon and put the rind in front and back of the right rear tire of his truck, when he would get ready to move it the motor would rev up but the truck wouldn't go anywhere, thinking something was wrong with the transmission he would get out and start looking to see what was wrong and would find the watermelon rind under the rear wheel, I would start laughing and he would start cursing. I was always doing crazy things for fun; sometimes it wouldn't be as funny to others as it was to me.

We would always have to shuck corn to feed the mules. We would shuck a burlap sack full at the time and would normally give each mule seven or eight ears of corn in the evening and a bundle of fodder and most of the time a tap of hay that had been baled, which was about six inches thick off the end of a square bale. We also had a water trough with water always available. I was told to always keep plenty of food and water where they could get it when they needed it. I can hear the mules today as they would bite into an ear of corn and start grinding it up with their teeth, that's a sound you wan't forget. There are so many memories of the past, some good and some bad that I can remember, and wonder how we would have felt if we had the things back then that we have today.

We would have to clean out the mule stalls. The manure would sometimes be packed so hard where the mules had walked on it that we would have to break it up with a pick and shovel it out the stall door onto a sled with side boards installed, and the mule would pull it to the garden or the field where we would spread it. Today they are cleaned out with a front end loader that made it much easier. We always used the manure for fertilizer for the gardens and to spread on the fields. Work on a farm was never ending, all our work was done by hand, we didn't have a tractor, and all our plowing in the fields was done with the mules as we walked behind the plows. Once you learned to plow you could follow the plow and use one hand on the plow handles and make it move the way you wanted, everything would come natural.

Our yards were sandy with no grass; we had several large china trees for shade. We would use brooms made with dog fennels and tied in bunches with cotton twine to sweep the sandy yards. It was always hard to keep the leaves and the china berries up when they started falling, going bare foot and walking on these berries were painful, really hard on your feet especially if you were barefoot because the berries were hard and would roll like ball bearings when you stepped on them. I remember my great grandfather would set under a china tree in the summer and when a thunder storm started coming up it was hard to get him to come in the house. It would take him longer to get in the house because of his disability from a stroke he had earlier and was paralyzed on one side. But he would wait until the last minute before he started getting out of the weather with lighting striking all around. That always frightened me because I was always afraid of thunder storms.

My aunt would sweep the wood floors in the house with brooms made with broom straw we gathered from the fields in the fall. Once a month our floors were scrubbed with a scoring broom that were made with a block of wood with holes bored in it and wet corn shucks pulled through the holes. My aunt Lara would get a tub of water, add homemade soap to the water and submerge the scouring broom in the water and scrub the floors until they looked like new, after they were clean she would use a mop made of cloth rags to dry the floor. I remember there were cracks in the floor that were large enough you could see the chickens walking under the house. The floors were made with pine boards and over time the boards would shrink causing cracks between them. They looked good when cleaned, but the cracks between the boards didn't help when it got cold in winter.

The soap we used to wash clothes were homemade, we would use animal fat and lye cooked in a wash pot and let stand until it cooled, the soap would come to the top and get hard when it cooled where it could be cut in pieces. These pieces of soap were used in the wash pot when our clothe were being boiled, and after being boiled they were washed in a tub to get the soap out and hung on a clothe line to dry in the sun. Lye soap was very harsh to your hands but would get the clothes clean. The only soap we would buy was soap to bathe with and clean our hands and wash dishes.

In the sand hills you would get very dirty working in the fields and had to take a bath every night, and with no running water or a way to heat it, you had to use a large wash tub of water drown from the well, we would leave the water in the sun to get warm in the summer, and in winter we would have to heat water in a kettle and pour it in the tub. You never went to bed on my aunts sheets dirty or you were in trouble. I remember after going barefoot in the fields my feet would be so black with dirt from walking in the black soil that I would have to scrub them to get them clean.

My aunt Lara washed all the clothes, swept and scrubbed the floors, canning food for winter, cooking all our food and working in the fields when she had time. When she washed our clothe she used a wash pot and boiled the clothe until they were clean, using lye soap that we made, removed them from the pot and wrenched them in clean water, by having no running water in the house and no electricity, we didn't have hot water, so she had to heat the water in the wash pot outside. If they didn't come clean by boiling them she would use a scrub board and scrub then by hand until all the dirt come out.

My aunt Lara could cook some of the best collards greens I ever eat, she would go to the garden and get the collard leaves, wash them and cook them in a pot with a piece of pork for seasoning, and adding a small amount of salt, stacking them in the pot with the leaves whole and cooking until they were tender, she said cooking them whole would keep the flavor in while they were cooking, and then she would take them out of the pot and cut them with a knife as she held them with a fork. The collards would be strong, but the flavor was great. She would also cook bread in a frying pan, called hoe cakes; they would be cooked like biscuits but in a pan sized cake. I would always look for the piece of pork she used for seasoning the collards and the streaked meat that would be attached to it, that was a treat.

She would also gather and cook turnips and greens which we grew in the fall and winter, that were always very good and was cooked with the same seasoning that gave them the flavor. She would also can them in jars for summer when we didn't have any growing. It was amazing what this woman could cook and preserve for later. She was always a very nice person but if she was crossed she could stand her ground.

When I was growing up we would sleep on a bed that had the mattress filled with straw that went on bottom of the bed, and one filled with cotton that went on top. My aunt Lara would make all the bed clothe including the mattress, She would take two large sheets made of cloth and sew them together making a sack called a bed tick, and fill one with straw and the other with cotton, the straw would go on the bottom and the cotton on top. She used a long needle to tack them together in about eight inch squares over the whole mattress, she then made the bed sheets out of whatever cloth she could get, she made the pillows and stuffed them with cotton, and made pillow cases to go over them, all of this were handmade. Her job was never ending and she never complained but expected others to do their share. I was blessed to be raised by people with the respect and care and love that my family had.

In the spring I always looked forward to the first of May, that was when I could start going barefoot, I would have to look over the yard vary closely for any glass or anything that could cut your feet while barefoot, that was always my job. I would go barefoot through the summer and late into September. One of the things that were bad about going barefoot was sand spurs. In the sandy land sand spurs was very common, and if you stepped on one it was hard to pull out because it had spurs on it that would go in and when you tried to pull it out it would hang like a fish hook and hurt really bad.

We would get one pair of shoes a year, and they had to do until the next year, if they got holes in the sols my uncle Mack would replace the sols and the heals if necessary, he would also buy heal taps that could be nailed to the heal of the shoe with small shoe nails to help keep them from wearing out, they were made of steel and you could hear a person walking across the floor with the steel taps on their shoes.

Our clothe would most always have patches on the knees were we would wear holes in them by doing a lot of things on our knees like putting out plants or picking cotton, I always had to keep my better clothe for school and Sunday, it would keep my aunt Lara busy washing and repairing our clothe, along with all her other chores. She would always say you might not have the best clothe, but you can always keep them clean and she lived by that motto. As I look back at the way we had to live in those days it makes me respect what people had to go through, but it also makes me proud that I was able to learn the lessons that you can only learn by going through the times we had to go through, and at that time it was a way of life for almost everybody.

I remember all our chairs in the kitchen were homemade with wood slat bottoms that were made with white oak strips and woven in, making a soft seat. We had a neighbor, Mr. Boone, who would come to your house and bottom chairs when they wore out, he would go to the woods and find a good straight white oak tree with no knots and split it, and with a drawing knife, cut long strips of wood and scrape them to the right size using a knife until he got the strips the way he wanted them, He would put the strips in a tub of hot water and let it soak overnight. The next day he would weave the strips in the chair bottom and let it dry, he was the best around at bottoming chairs. And could tell some of the funniest stories as he worked on the chairs that would always keep you laughing. He was a good man.

We all drink coffee in the morning, I always drink mine black, My uncle Mack, always drink hot water boiled in a kettle and drank it hot like coffee, I could never understand why he would drink hot water, all other times during the day he drink cool water, never milk or any other drinks. I had a hard time understanding why he drank hot water. He had his strange ways. He always would take a half gallon jar of water with him to the field and put it in a shade at the end of the rows where he was plowing, so when he got thirsty he had his water.

I remember at Christmas my aunt would cook cakes, pies and egg custards, and fill the pie safe with them a few days before Christmas and we weren't allowed to touch them until Christmas day. We would get a few oranges and apples, some candy, and sometimes a wood crate of 24 Coca Colas, Pepsi Colas; or orange crush, which was always a treat. There was very little money to buy presents but everybody was happy and didn't expect anything else, when I was small I would always get one toy and I always was excited on Christmas morning when I got my toy.

I remember going in the woods with my aunt looking for old forest pine that had fell on the ground many years earlier for fire starter, she would take an axe to cut all of the outside wood off to get to the heart of the tree and get the heart and split it to start fires and put it in a sack to carry it home. The heart would have so much tar in it you could start a fire almost as good as using kerosene, back then it was called "fat lightered", when it got cold in winter you needed something to start a fire as quick as possible, and the heart pine would burn for a long time getting the regular wood started. We would also find a stump where the tree had been gone for a long time and the wood had rotted away from the stump leaving the heart intact, we would cut and split the heart and gather it for the rich wood for fire starter. To think back today it's amazing what we had to do to stay warm and survive in the winter, and all our neighbors had to do the same.

After I got old enough I had to help cut and gather wood for the cook stove for cooking and the fireplace for heating in winter. We would go to the woods and cut, haul and, stack enough wood on the back porch to last all winter. We would always try to cut oak because it would burn longer and put out a lot more heat. To make some extra money my uncle would go to the woods and cut a pickup truck load of oak wood, and carry it to Pageland and sell it, in the winter there were always someone wanting to buy fire wood, and he had his regular customers that would buy several loads per year.

By cutting and selling wood would help us buy the things we needed like flour, coffee and sugar. We were fortunate to have enough wooded land to be able to cut wood for our use and sell some to help out. In those days you had plenty to do in the winter as well as summer, there was never a time to set down and relax without thinking about what you could do to help make ends meet, which was the reality of living on a small farm in the 1940's. I know that's the reason I value money so much today, because when I was growing up we had to struggle in order to make ends meet with very little money, and I can't get it out of my way of living to this day. I'm always looking at prices any time I go to the grocery store, a few cents here and a few cents there will add up. I can't get that mind set out of my head.

We would always hunt a lot in the winter. We would build rabbit boxes and set then in the evening around the edges of the woods, and make rounds the next morning to collect any rabbit's we might have caught that night, we might have eight or ten boxes to check, some mornings we would have a possum in one of the boxes with a rabbet in another, We didn't eat possums but we had some friends that did and would give them the possums. When we cough a possum in the rabbet box we would have to get the scent of the possum out of the box or a rabbit wouldn't go in it. We would burn pine straw in the rabbet box to eliminate the scent. The rabbets we cough would be butchered and cooked for food, and if we had more then we needed we would save them to butcher later or give them to a neighbor. Back in those days we had no deer in our area. We never hunted for sports and never wasted any food. This was the way we survived. Some people today will say this is inhumane, but they will go to the grocery store and buy all kind of meat and think nothing about it. I guess it alright with them if someone kills them in a commercial establishment where in some cases is more inhumane. Maybe they should visit a butcher house and see how they kill and prepare the meat you buy in the stores. It might change their way of thinking.

When it was cold in winter I would come in the house and stand with my back to the open fire place to get warm, one day I was standing close to the fire when I heard a loud sound and hot colds popped out on the floor, I thought it was unusual for the wood to pop that bad, and after sweeping the colds back in the fireplace I felt something sharp in the leg seam of my blue jeans, after father investigation I found it was a 22 caliber shell casing embedded in the fabric seam, I had lost one of my bullets on the floor and my aunt had sweep it in the fireplace without seeing it. If it been one inch over it would have hit me in my leg and with that force would have embedded itself in my leg. The weight of the lead bullet had forced the shell casing to fly out.

We would fish in the spring and summer in a small creek, called Black Creek, this creek had some deep holes and a lot of catfish and perch, We would often sane the deep holes with a net and catch a lot of red breast perch, that were large and good eating fish. We would also set fish hooks at night for catfish up and down the creek, and then go back up and down the creek checking to see what we cough. The hooks were set using a hook and sinker on a line tied to a short pole, stuck in the bank, with a lantern you could walk up and down the creek and see the end of the pole going up and down when a fish got cough. Sometime we would catch an ell that was my uncle Macks favorite fish.

I come up with what I thought was a better idea, why not get in the water and grabble under the rocks and in holes in the banks, and I began to catch a lot of fish of all types, catfish, bream, ells, and mud suckers until I pulled a snake out, that was the end of my grabbling.

In those days it was hard to find fresh fish in stores mostly because it was hard to keep them without much way to keep them from spoiling in stores. About the only time you could find fresh fish in stores were when a batch would be brought in from the beach packed in ice, and they didn't last very long. The only fish you could find plenty of was salt fish that were preserved in salt brain in a wooden barrel, but you would need to soak them over night to get most of the salt out before cooking. But when you eat a lot of salt fish you would drink water until you thought you were going to get waterlogged, that's how thirsty salt fish would make you.

One time a friend and I were going fishing in a pond nearby, they were lots of bream in this pond, mostly small but were good eating. We had to go through a pasture where there were several cows and one large bull, we had been through this pasture several times before and never saw the bull but this time I saw him looking at us and said to my friend, that bull don't like us, and he said don't worry he want bother us, and we continued through the pasture and got almost to the other side of the fence when I heard the bull make a loud snort and he started pawing the ground and coming toward us, and we started running and jumped over the fence, and I got hung in the barbwire and had to tear my pants almost off and cut my leg to get over the fence, the bull stopped at the fence and stood there pounded on the ground with his feet and snorting as long as he could see us as we run away, we never went back through that pasture any more.

Back in those days food were a top priority and you didn't waste anything that could be eat, if you could not use it there was always neighbors that would love to have it, and we always remembered our neighbors when we had something extra, and they would remember us as well when they had extras.

Life were hard in the 1940s and 50s, but there were good times as well and there were no pressure on you as long as you did your share of daily chores. For a 100 lb kid caring a 5 gallon bucket of water aproxly 100 yards from the well to the water troughs for the mules, and then we had to put there feed in the stalls for them to eat when they wanted, it were quite a chore, but it was necessary and had to be done daily. Our animals would get their food and water most of the time before we got ours.

When I was small my breakfast in the morning were mostly a mound of sugar in a saucer with coffee poured in the middle and soaked up with bread and eat along with a fried egg, it is now said that a lot of sugar is not good for you, but it was good for energy then and I am still going at nearly eighty. Other food that's not good for you is a lot of animal fat "pure lard", I grew up eating everything seasoned with pure lard, and you can't get more animal fat then pure lard. When we butchered our hogs in the fall and winter we would always used the side meat to fry out and make lard, we never used it to make bacon, because we needed the lard more for use later on in the year.

You had to eat what you had because you didn't have money to by what were called healthy food, even if you could find it. That's why hunting animals for food were so impotent. When we killed animals in those times it was for food not sports. In those days for some reason we never raised cows or had beef. I can remember the first beef I ever eat, I was about ten years old when a school friend and I went to a café in Pageland SC, and he offered to buy me some lunch, and we got stew beef and rice which cost one dollar per plate., and we got a plate rounded full, From then on all I ever wanted was stew beef and rice and would go back to that café every time I got a chance and had the money for more stew beef and rice. I still love stew beef and rice today.

If we needed milk we would get it from our neighbor who had several cows. My aunt Lara would go to the neighbors, Mr. and Mrs. Jordon and get milk for me when I was small, I remember watching Mrs. Jordan milk the cows, setting on a stool and using both hands, you could hear the milk hitting the bottom of the steel bucket with a lot of pressure, that sound I'll never forget. I guess that's why I don't drink milk today, because I drink so much when I was young. We lived a simple life and always helped our neighbors when they needed us and they helped us as well. That was the way people survived in the country in those days. If a neighbor got sick or hurt the people in the community would come in and help with whatever needed to be done until he was able to return to doing his work, and there was never any charge for any work they done. They would even cultivate his fields when needed. We never had very much except the friendship of each other. Everybody would help each other when needed.

Our young neighbors a little older than me would go to a pond in the summer when it was very hot to swim, they would stop by my house and pick me up and I would go along, I remember they had a Chevrolet pickup and they would have the tail gate down and we would ride on it about four miles to the pond where the water were real cool by being spring fed. That was how I learned to swim by watching them. One of the girls was about four years older than me and was a good swimmer and could float on her back, which I never could do, she helped me learn to swim, and the cool water would always feel good when it was hot.

When I was small, about eight years old I would play on a mowing machine that was always parked by the mule fence and next to the road, I would pretend I was mowing hay, we used the mowing machine to cut hay in the summer and rake and stack it when it got dry. I was playing on the mowing machine one day when I saw something flying around, I didn't pay it much attention not knowing they were hornets, when all of a sudden something hit me between the eyes and knocked me off the mowing machine and when I fell and looked up I saw a big hornets' nest hanging in the tree over the mowing machine, and hornets flying everywhere, When I finely got up and started running they started chasing me, they followed me all the way around the house until I finely went in the back door and got away, my head were hurting bad and I had a small hole directly between my eyes where the hornet stung me, and to this day the scar is still visible. I was always told that a hornet would aim at a point between your eyes to sting, I learned that day how true it was and still have the scar to prove it. I learned to always keep my eyes open and look for wasp or hornet nest where ever I might be.

Another time I got in trouble was when we visited a friend's house that had bought a new washing machine with a ringer attachment on the top. After you washed the clothes you could start the clothe in the ringer and it would pull them through the rollers and squeeze out the water, after she showed us all the features and told us how good it worked, they turned away talking about other things, she didn't turn the machine off and I was watching the rollers turn and started to let my fingers rub on them, when all of a sudden the rollers cough my fingers and pulled my hand into the rollers, when my fingers were pulled in my thumb caught on the frame and the rollers started to spin on the back of my hand, I hollered and the lady turned and saw what had happened and hit the release lever and I pulled my hand out, all the skin was peeled off the back of my hand where the rollers had spun and my hand looked really bad but there were no broken bones, so they bandaged it up and I had a real sore hand for several days and when it healed it left a scar about an inch long and ½ inch wide that I had for several years. From that moment on I would never let my hands get close to a roller of any kind moving.

I remember when I saw my first television, I was about ten or eleven years old as best as I can remember, when a neighbor close by bought a new television set, the first in our part of the country that I were aware of, we were invited to their house to watch the television shortly after they bought it. It was the most amazing thing I had ever seen. I remember it had a large alumna antanner on top of the house with a lot of small pipe pointing out on both sides, and if the picture wasn't clear enough to watch he would climb on the house and move it until it got clearer. That was an experience I'll always remember. We watched it for hours before we had to go home. It was very entertaining.

When I was a young kid our neighbor who was an amateur photogher would use a hawk eye camera to take pictures, he would go home and develop, and print them, he saw my interest in the process and invited me to come to his house and watch him develop the pictures. I got so interested in watching him develop the film and let them dry, then use a projector to transfer the image to photo paper and develop it into a photograph, I found where I could buy the paper and chemicals which was not expensive, and made my own projector and started working with the process myself using a 6 volt battery to power a projector I had made. I didn't do this for anybody else, only to get the satisfaction of doing it myself. I always believed I could do anything anybody else could do, maybe not as good but I could do it and get better with time and practices.

I have always believed you can do anything you want to if you put your heart in it. It's all in your frame of mind. I think what helped me have this feeling is because of the way I grew up not being able to buy what was needed and having to make it out of whatever was available. These lessons I learned will always stay with me.

When I was in my early teens I had a 1937 Chevrolet pickup that I would drive to Pageland to work when I worked at the garage, I didn't have any drivers license because I was not old enough to get them, but I needed to get to work so I traded a motor bike for this old pickup and it run pretty good until the gas tank got so much trash in it that I couldn't keep it running. I got a piece of copper tubing and a five gallon gas can, rigged a line from the can to the fuel pump and set the can in the floor on the passenger side and continued to drive to work and back for several months. Back then there was not much traffic on the road and you never saw a highway patrol, the only problem was the gas odor inside the cab, you had to drive with the windows down to stand the odor, I was told that I were going to blow the truck up and kill myself, but I would never smoke while I was in the cab, I had to do whatever I needed to do to get to work, I can only imagine what would happen if caught doing that today. Back then the traffic were no way like it is today; you could drive some days from my house the seven miles plus to the shop where I without seeing a single car. When I look back now I can see where I did foolish things. Thankfully after driving from about twelve years old until I got my license I never got a ticket. I can tell someone today the truth about how it was back then, but they don't want to believe it could have been that bad, Things has changed that much.

Where I live now, in the panhandle of Lancaster county and have lived here for over 50 years, I've seen this part of the county go from corn fields to a four lane highway with business on every corner and still growing, this was unthinkable in the 1960's I always dreaded to go to charlotte because of traffic, and now at the end of the road from my house is as bad as it was in charlotte back then. The amazing thing is I can drive fifty miles south to below Pageland S C and the country is the same as it was over fifty years ago except for county water and cable TV, the development has not reached that for south, but it's on the way.

Back when I was in my early teens I had learned to play a guitar and every week end some friends and I would go to someone's house and play music, and there was always some girls that would like to sing, this went on for a long time until I was cutting on a piece of wood with a sharp wood chisel one day, and hit the chisel with my right hand to drive it in the wood and it slipped and the chisel blade hit my index finger on my left hand and cut it to the bone, and I could see the ligaments cut completely into, I could see them in the slice where the finger was cut. I bandaged up the finger and let it heal on its own; never went to a doctor, knowing it needed to be fixed, but back then you never went to a doctor unless it was a matter of life or death. With the ligaments being cut

I couldn't close my finger completely for years after it healed and had no control over that finger, it being on my left hand I couldn't play the guitar any more because I couldn't make the cords. It took over twenty five years for me to get full control of my finger again but somehow they grew back and I can use my finger again. I still have the scar on my finger where it was cut. I had a lot of things happen to me while I was growing up but all of these things that happened taught me lessons to be more careful at anything I did.

I was in my early teens when on Saturday nights a group would get together and get some beer and go out on the dirt roads find a place to park, drink beer and have fun. One night we were out with a bunch of girls and guys drinking beer, none of us were of drinking age but we could always buy beer at a country store, with no questions asked. I was never one to drink a lot of beer because I didn't like the taste of it. But this night someone had got a pint of mint Gen and asked if I would like to try it and I did, I thought it tasted pretty good, and started to sip on it not knowing you were supposed use it in a mixed drink; I kept drinking it straight out of the bottle. I were setting on the ditch bank at a cross road where everybody were just drinking and having fun when I noticed I were feeling kindly strange and started to get up and move around, my legs wouldn't move no matter how hard I tried, and I was that way for several hours, while everybody laughed at me, the bad part I didn't pass out, and I knew everything that were going on but could not get up or move around. After that I never touched gen again, not even in a mixed drink. I guess that was a good lesson to learn.

I was about twelve years old when a school friend of mine about a year older than me were trying to find a way to make some money and my uncle Mack overheard us talking about it and suggested we cut some pulp wood on a section of his woods that had a large amount of pine trees, he said we could use his cross cut saw and axes to cut the pulp wood, we decided to do it. We had never cut that much wood before but we would do it as long as we could make money. Using a cross cut saw wasn't an easy job you had to have one person on each end and would have to pull the saw back and forward until you cut the log off, if each person wasn't pulling and pushing together you would work yourself to death and get nowhere. We finely got things working and continued to cut down and cut up the pulp wood logs, each one had to be eight foot long, so we measured and cut a stick eight foot long to measure with and we would made a mark with the axe at the end of the stick. After cutting several logs of wood the saw got where it wouldn't cut, so we would have to sharpen it with a file and then it would cut but would stick about half way through the wood, so we asked my uncle why the saw was sticking and he said we were learning how the saw worked, you have to set the teeth after sharpening to drag the saw dust out and use some kerosene on the blade to help keep it from sticking, we got a glass drink bottle, filled it with kerosene and stuck a small pine top it the top of the bottle and after cutting a log off we would wipe the saw with the kerosene and had no other cutting problems. After cutting down and cutting up several trees we would stack the logs and look at the stack and wonder when we would ever get a load, we needed at least two cords for a truck load, and we had only about a quarter cord, so we found out we had a job in front of us. We continued to cut and stack until we got what we thought were a load, and got the hauler to come by and look at it and said it would be close but he would haul it. After this load that was the end of us cutting pulp wood.

When I were about sixteen years old and had just got my licenses, a man was cutting pulp wood on our property and had to haul it to a wood yard in Patrick SC about thirty miles away. He had a 1947 Chevrolet two ton truck and asked if I would drive his truck to the wood yard, he was afraid to drive it with a large load that high, the pulp wood would be stacked about three foot above the top of the cab, making it real top heavy, you had to be careful with it that high, not only watch for low power lines over head but you had to make sure you were going slow on curves. At about that time the federal government had just passed a law that anyone under 17 years old could not do any work involved with anything the government had to do with, and the government bought products from this wood yard, I had heard about this law and told him that I wasn't old enough to pass the age requirements, If they looked at you and you didn't look over 17 they would require proof of age or they wouldn't buy the wood you had, so I told him I would drive the truck close to the wood yard and get out, he could drive in the lot sell the wood and pick me up when he got out. At 16 years old, I hauled several loads of pulp wood for him and he would pay me for driving. It was scary mostly going down hills but I never had any problems and he would pay me to drive the truck. There were no requirements for CDL license back then.

I have always believed you can do anything if you really want to, you can find a way if you look hard enough.

I remember the world war two ration stamps, not to be confused with today's food stamps, and I remember solders training in our part of the country, there would be Jeeps, trucks and lots of solders around our house playing war games. They would be reds and blues and would wear a band around their arms above their elbows to distinguish the side they were on. And a sergeant would grade them on there progress. Any waste they had left over were buried, they left nothing behind to be seen. When all the games were over someone from the Army would visit the site and check for any damage that had been done to your property and a month or so later the government would send a check to pay for it. I was very young and this was excitement for me to watch.

You had to have ration stamps to buy sugar, coffee and many other things during the war, I was only about three or four years old when I would get hold of the stamp books and play with the stamps, always losing some and getting in trouble. The stamps were mailed to each family once a month. Some people would trade stamps that they didn't use or need to others for deferent things. Which was illegal? If you went to a store to buy something and didn't have a stamp for that product, by law they could not sell it to you. It is hard for the younger generation todayy to understand what it was like in the country on a farm in the 1940's in war time. Neighbors always looked out for each other. I still have the certificate that the aguculture department issued to my uncle so he could present it to a dealer that gave him permission to buy a pickup truck for use on the farm, but he never used it because he didn't have the money to buy it.

Back then you didn't need locks on your doors because if someone was caught stealing and convicted they went to the chain gang with hard work, and it didn't take eight or ten months to go to trial. They were tried quickly and if convicted they went straight to the chain gang.

When I were about five years old my uncle Mack rented the house where I was born, an old house with four rooms, along with a few acres of land to a young black family with two children about my age, they moved in and farmed the land, growing cotton, corn, watermelons, an several smaller crops. He would pay the rent in the fall when his crops were sold. He didn't have money to pay in advance and wasn't expected to. I had never heard the word racist nor had any feeling of them being different except their skin being darker, we worked together in the fields, visited each other in our homes and played together, and until this day we feel like brothers and sisters. They were hard working people. They raised sugar cane on some of the land each year, and would take the stalks to a cane mill to get the juice to make molasses. He was the best at cooking molasses as anybody I have ever seen. He would put the molasses in glass jars after they were cooked a sell them to make extra money.

I remember one day this man were plowing in the field when he saw a large black snake commonly called a black runner, he was so afraid of snakes, he dropped the plow and started running with the snake chasing him, he ran until he got tired and stopped to challenge the snake, when he did the snake started running from him, they chased each other back and forward until the snake finely decided to keep going and got away. In the sand hills it was common for a black snake to chase you, but if you turned and run at them, the snake would turn and run from you. He said he had never had a snake chase him before.

I always wanted to try deferent things, like when I was at my grand fathers house on a Sunday afternoon and my uncle Junior had an old Harley Davidson motor cycle it was old, heavy and I remember it had a full sized car battery under the seat between your legs, I was about five foot three and weighted about one hundred and five lb at that time. but I wanted to ride that motorcycle. The road by the house were dirt and very sandy, my uncle Junior held the bike up for me to get on it and I started up the road, ever thing were going good, but when I tried to turn around to come back it laid down, and somehow the throttle were still open and it started spinning around on the ground, I didn't have enough weight to control it so I were followering it and trying to stay out of its way until some of the guys could run up the road and got it stopped. From that time on I had very little interest in motorcycles.

I have always loved to build things and make them do a job that there were no tools available to do, and have made a lot of things, some worked great and some not so great but I would always find a way to improve the ones that didn't work so good. I remember when my son Robby and I were working on an oil filter wrench and went through about seventeen prototypes before we finely got it to work the way we thought it should, and after we got it to work the way it should we applied for and received a united states patent on it and made and sold a lot of them through catalogs. We designed and built several other devices to do a job that we needed to do and no tools to do them, I have always believed if you needed a tool to do something and one was not available to buy, and then built your own. When we were doing repairs in the textile industries, we designed and built many tools that was needed to do different types of work and we had to design and make them all ourself.

In the hot summer we would lower our spoilable food in the well to keep it cool because we had no refrigerator or electricity, the well being about sixty foot deep it was very cool at the bottom when it was hot during the day outside.

On wet days when it was too wet to work in the fields, several friends would get together for a squirrel hunt; they would hunt a radius of several miles and hunt all day, and when they come home in the evening they would put their entire kill on a table and skin and prepare them for cooking, after they were all cleaned they would be divided equally with each family.

One day I was hunting alone when I saw a squirrel go in a hole in a hollow tree, I decided to run my hand up the hole and try to catch it by the tail and pull it out; I felt his tail and finely got a good grip on it and started to pull. My fingers would slip off and I would get another grip and pull again, finely I could hear and feel his claws scratching the inside of the tree as it was being pulled out, and all of a sudden I pulled the squirrel out, and when it come out it wrapped around my hand and started biting, scratching, as I was slinging my hand as hard as I could to get it loose, but that squirrel held on and kept on biting and scratching until I finely slung it loose and it went up another tree, my hand were pouring blood with cuts all over it, it looked like it had been cut with a knife. My aunt Lara would always make me carry a hankcufte that was about 14 inches square that she had made, I used it to wrap up my hand and stop the bleeding until I could get home and put some alcohol on it and a bandage. That was the end of me pulling an animal out of a hole in a hollow tree.

On Saturdays a group of us would get together and have a shooting contest with rifles and shotguns. We would set up targets consisting of several deferent type, we would have some for rifles and some for shotguns, the rifles targets would be a sewing thread starched between two post about six foot apart and at fifteen foot away you would try to cut the thread with the bullet, we would always use the same rifle and the same ammunition out of the same box. We would mostly use the 22 Winchester single shot that I always used for hunting and I had a lot of practice with it, and would often win. another target was to stick a strike anywhere match up at the same distance away and try to cut off the head of the match off, or better strike it an leave the stem standing, that was very hard to do, but it could be done. All of this shooting had to be done without using anything to help steady the gun; you had to stand on both feet without leaning on anything. When we used the shot gun the rules were same except we would have a target nailed to a tree with a bulls eye drawn in the center and you would have to be thirty feet away, using the same gun, and same shells you would try to get as many shots in the target and as close to the bulls eye as possible, who ever won in these classes would have bragging rights until the next time. I was always good with the rifle but the shot gun was never my thing. My uncle Mack would almost always win the shot gun class. We had a lot of fun and it were a good way to pass the time and visit with our friends; there were not much to do in those days except working and taking care of the chores around the farm.

I was around eleven years old when I saw my first movie at a theater in Pageland SC. I went to the movie with my uncle Pete, all I can remember about the movie was it was a western with Wild Bill Elliott and his side kicks Jingles. It was fascinating for me because I had never seen anything on a big screen with that loud noise and action; and Jingles was so funny I couldn't stop laughing, I think it cost 12cents each to get in. after that I went ever chance I got. Being a small guy I didn't look my age and continued to pay 12 cents until I was around 14 years old, I would always say twelve when they asked my age, I didn't think I was lying because I was twelve but I didn't tell them I were over, until one Saturday the owner told me the next time I had to pay adult price, she knew I was over twelve, and I said "yes mam".

We never complained because we knew it was all we could afford.

We lived on food we grew on the farm the family had owned for generations other then flour, sugar, and coffee all other food were grown on the farm. we didn't have money to buy extras other than what was necessary, most our food were grown and canned for winter use, Hogs were raised and butchered for meat and cured in a smoke house from year to year. If we had chicken on Sunday's we would have to catch one off the yard and kill and clean them. Although we had very little, we had love and respect for each other.

We had four large fig trees in our back yard and the figs would get ripe around mid June. For extra money we would pick and sell the figs for fifty cents per peck, and we could pick them about every two days until they were all gone, I was light, less than 100 pound and would climb the trees and pick the figs in the top of the trees, sometimes we would get six or seven pecks, what we did not sell my aunt Lara would make fig preserves and can them. We never let anything go to waste,

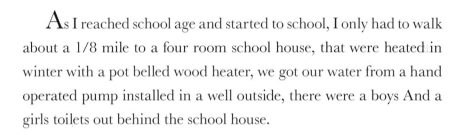

As I reached school age and started to school, I only had to walk about a 1/8 mile to a four room school house, that were heated in winter with a pot belled wood heater, we got our water from a hand operated pump installed in a well outside, there were a boys And a girls toilets out behind the school house.

When I was in about the third grade, I would sneak some of my great grand father's pipe tobacco out of the house and take it to school, at recess me and a bunch of my friends would get together on the outside and roll and smoke cigarettes out of the tobacco. He always would buy golden grain tobacco in twelve pack cases, they come in small sacks with a pack of cigarette papers glued to the back, I learned to roll cigarettes almost as good as a machine, so I had to roll everybody's for them. That tobacco was so fine that if a puff of wind comes by you didn't have any tobacco left and had to start over. There were woods behind the school and that is where we would go to smoke, the toilets were also in the edge of the woods, one day we were smoking and somehow started a fire in the toilet and we run to tell the teacher that the toilet was on fire, she got the fire out and checked everybody's pockets for matches and never found any, and never found out how the fire got started.

At recess we would play cowboy and Indians behind the school in the woods, we Built play houses by cutting down small trees and using them to make a frame and cover it with pine straw, sometimes we would have several of them through the woods, being the fire hazard they was its amazing we didn't get them on fire by smoking, I guess we learned our lesson from setting the toilet on fire earlier and having to tell the teacher. We used our play houses for the complete school year. The girls would always come around giggling and making fun of us, but we all looked forward to recess and no one was bullies that tried to cause trouble, I can only imagine what it would be like today.

After the sand pit opened behind the school we would go to the sand pit and have dirt ball fights, we would find a stash of red dirt balls and throw them at each other and try to hit them anywhere except the head, the sand balls would burst when it hit something, but sometime you would get one that had clay mixed in, they wouldn't break up and the person that got hit was in trouble and would start looking for a rock to retaliate, but this didn't happen very often. Everybody at school knew each other and their parents knew each other as well and no one wanted their parents to be told about some stupid thing they had done. In those days kids would play together and have fun without being mean to each other because they knew their parents would not tolerate it.

I had a friend at school who would drive a Model A Ford four door sedan to school that his dad owned, he was only about 13 years old and was kind of wild with that old car, one day there were about six of us in that Model A as we went down a narrow dirt road with a sharp left curve at the sand pit, I was sitting in the rear left side when he approached the curve and I could feel both left side wheels come off the ground as he tried to turn left, the car seemed to get on those two wheels and just stay there until it finely dropped back on all four wheels, it scared us all bad enough that we never tried to take a curve that fast any more. If it had continued to turn over we would have rolled down a steep bank and in a hole about thirty foot deep, that had been dug out for the sand pit, and I might not be writing this now.

When I was about ten years old I was smoking regular, but for years I would not let my uncle Mack see me smoke, after about twelve years old I started smoking Prince Albert Tobacco and continued until about fourteen and started buying Pall Mall cigarettes when I began working at a garage, and continued to smoke none filters cigarettes until June 2, 1992 when I quit for good. In the mid 1950's you could buy cigarettes for 20 cents a pack, when I quit they had gone to over 50 cents a pack. I was working late in our shop on the night of June 2nd 1992 when I realized it was 9:45 and I only had three cigarettes left, and the country store close which was close by closed at 10:00 o'clock. I went to the house set down at the kitchen table and started thinking, cigarettes are getting higher by the day and I knew they were not good for my health, but the most important thing was they were controlling me, and I would not let nothing control me, so I put the three cigarettes I had on the dresser top in the bed room and about three days later my wife put then in the trash can, and I have never smoked another one from that day own. I will have to admit I chewed a lot of chewing gum for the next several months. You can always do anything if you make up your mind too.

For six years, I attended this school and finished the sixth grade, which was all my formal education.

Each day except Saturday and Sunday after school I would walk home changed out of my school clothes, went to the fields, and worked until Sundown, at 10 years old I was plowing in the fields with a mule named Bell, We raised cotton, corn, watermelons, and always had a large garden with all kind of vegetables.

I remember when I was small My uncle Mack would go the the woods and cut a small hickory three to use to make axe handles and hammer handles, he would set in a chair by the fire place for several hours each night working on a handle, using a drawing knife to get the shape and then a pocket knife to scrape the fine details, this would be done while the wood was freshly cut so it would easy to work to shape, when he finished he would let it dry out and get hard. To put the axe on the handle he would put the axe in the fire place and cover it with hot coals and leave it there for several hours, and when he placed it on the handle it would start smoking as he submerged it in water to shrink the axe to the handle, that was a lot of work to replace an axe handle, but you didn't go buy one as long as you could make it. He would do the same with his plow handles and hammer handles, he would also make the single trees that were used to hook the mules to the plows, very little was bought. I learned a lot when I was young watching other people make things they needed to get a job done without having to buy things, because you really didn't have money to buy what you needed back then so you made it.

The only time I had to play as a kid was at school at recess and on Saturdays and Sundays during the week I had to help with chores and do whatever I could to help, and your chores always come first.

I wasn't the only kid that had to work, we all had to help out and no one complained.

When I was about six years old I would always have to carry fertilizer for my uncle to keep his fertilizer distributor full when he was putting fertilizer in the rows before planting. He would buy fertilizer in two hundred pound bags in the spring, we would use 2 hundred pound per acre and he would always order about two tons and the merchant would deliver it. When we got the land prepared and the rows laid off, he would load about three or four sacks on a sled and with a mule hooked to the sled would pull the fertilizer to the field and place the bags at deferent locations, someone would have to carry a bucket of fertilizer to him each time he made a trip to the end of one row and back on another. I was usually the fertilizer carrier and would meet him with a ten quart bucket full to refill the distributor, I would use a quart coffee can to fill the bucket while he was going to the end of the row and back, at six or seven years old that bucket was very heavy and he would have to walk around and dump it in the fertilizer distributor because I couldn't lift it high enough to dump. It might take a half a day to put out fertilizer in the field and then he would have to come back with a plow and cover the fertilizer before it rained and washed it away.

After preparing the ground and putting in the fertilizer you had just got started with growing a crop, you had to plant the cotton and corn and keep all the grass out, thin out the cotton to about six inches apart, after about three weeks after the plants come up we had to put out side dressing along beside the cotton, and corn as well. We would use what was called soda, which was nitrogen, by hand and come back with a plow and cover it up, this made the plants grow faster and turn a dark green, we then had to plow the crops to keep the grass from coming up chocking out the plants, we would have to plow the crops several times until you would lay by in late June and let it finish growing and bearing, then in early September we would start picking the cotton, pulling fodder and, gathering the corn.

We would always plant sweet potatoes, and as they grew you could watch the ground around the plants each day start to crack from day to day as the potatoes grew, and when the potatoes started to put on you could see them start pushing up the dirt from day to day, with sweet potatoes they would grow and get bigger until late fall when you would plow them up using what was called a middle buster, and then pick up all the potatoes and store them in a potato bed in the back yard, to make a potato bed you would dig a hole in the ground about two foot deep and three foot around, put pine needles in the hole about six inches thick and put the potatoes own top of the pine needles and cover the top with another foot of needles and build a mound of dirt on top of that, it would keep them from freezing in the winter and when you wanted potatoes you would use your hands and dig a hole just big enough to get your hand through and pull the potato's out, when you got all the potatoes out you needed you would cover the hole back up. The potatoes would keep and not freeze all winter and into the next spring. That's the only way we had to preserve the potatoes. We would also grow regular potatoes for baking and frying, but they were easier to keep as long as you would keep them in a cool dark place in the house.

We had several Muscadine and scuppernong vines both black and bronze, some people called them grapes, my aunt would make pies and jam from them and would can some every season for that winter, she would can them hole and when you opened them they tasted gust like when they come off the vine. I would always climb in the vines and eat them until I would almost pop. I liked them right off the vine. When they got ripe in early summer I would climb the vines

52

and set on top and eat muscadines until I couldn't hold any more, things like that is why spring and summer is my favorite time of year and why I have all kind of fruit trees and vines on my place today. The old saying is so true, you can take the man out of the country but you can't take the country out of the man.

We had a large mulberry tree in the middle of a field that would be loaded with berries each year, the only problem the tree were so tall we couldn't reach the berries and if they weren't picked before they got over ripe enough to fall off the birds would get them. So it was my job to climb the tree and shake the limbs hard enough to cause the berries to fall so we could pick them up, the mulberries was really good for pies and canning. We didn't let anything go to waste; we would find a way to get it. We also had a large apple tree in another field that always made large apples, I would eat some raw but they were sour and were best for canning. They had stripes around them and made good canned apples.

We would also go in the woods and find a hickory tree and look for hickory nuts that had fell on the ground, you could crack them and get the meat out of the shell, they were hard to crack but was real good the only problem was to get them before the squirrels got them.

We had two large walnut trees where we would gather walnuts to make pies and I would always get a hammer and a rock and sit down under the tree and crack and eat walnuts until I would get the stomach ache, there was nothing like fresh cracked walnuts although they weren't easy to get out of the shell.

In mid summer we would go in the woods where they were a lot of trees called blackjack oak, the ground were sandy and there were a lot of hack berries trees growing wild mixed in with the blackjack, a hack berry was kind of like a blue berry except a lot smaller and not as sweet, we would pick them and my aunt Lara would make hack berry pies or jelly, the only problem was with them not being as sweet as blue berries it took a lot of sugar to get them sweet, but they were plentiful and not hard to pick. In those days you would always look for anything you could use for food. In the sand hills a few miles south of us they were blue berries growing wild, but not as many as there were hack berries.

In the spring we would go close to the North Carolina state line about eight miles away where there were cresses greens growing wild in the fields. We would gather the greens and my aunt Lara would cook them like mustard greens or turnips greens, they were good but had a different taste. We also would find young poke salad in the spring and she would cook it, I would eat it but it had a really strong taste. We ate a lot of things that people today would not think of eating.

We always raised hogs during the year for meat, and would feed them with anything we had, including corn, watermelons, cantaloupes and any table scraps. The more you fed them the fatter they would get, when the school was going on we would go to the school house every day and pick up the left over's and scrapes for the hogs. We would also go to a bakery in Monroe NC and get stale bread and sweets they had brought back in, hogs would eat anything and we usually had eight to ten to feed and mostly raised them from pigs.

It's hard for people today to realize the work that went into growing a crop to make a living, it was never ending. Today you have all kind of equipment to do these jobs and all you have to do is sit in a seat and drive the equipment. In the early days you had to do most work physically. With a lot of hard work involved.

There was a peach orchard beside the school house that were owned by one of our neighbors, when the peaches would get ripe I would sneak out of the woods and get a hand full of peaches and go back in the woods and eat them, they seemed to taste better when I got them that way.

What money we had come from the cotton, watermelons and any corn we didn't need to feed the animals or to be ground for corn meal. I was tough to always take good care of the animals, because they were the ones that helped us make our living by pulling the plows and doing the hard work that we couldn't do. You would always feed the mules good and always when it was very hot, stop and let them cool off before continuing on.

When I was about ten years old a man named Mr. Sellers bought a piece of land behind the school house and started a sand pit. He would have all the top soil pushed off and get the red sand to sell to construction companies to use to mix mouter for laying brick and making foundations, he had several big dump trucks that hauled it to places like Charlotte NC and other places. I had always been fascinated with caterpillars and bulldozers, and could set and watch them for hours, he had a man that operated a small dozer to clean off the small trees and remove the top soil, I would go in the evenings when I didn't have to work in the fields and set on a bank and watch him operate the dozer, sometimes I would go and watch two or three days a week after school, after several days he noticed me watching, and one day he stopped the dozer and motioned for me to come over, when I walked over he asked me why I was coming and watching him all the time, I said I liked to watch the bulldozer work. He slid back in the seat and told me to crawl up and set in front of his legs and he would let me drive it. I was all excited and road with him the rest of the day, he would drive the dozer and I would operate the blade. He told me to come back the next day after the owner left and he would let me do it again, and this went on until he finished doing all the grading, I got so good at keeping the blade level that he said I was as good as him. His name was Jim Stogner and we become good friends and he even come to my house and told my Uncle Mack and Aunt Lara what he had been doing and they become friends as well.

One of my child hood friends father had two tractors, a B Alice chamber and a CA Alice chamber, My uncle Mack had haired him to do some plowing, getting the fields ready for the spring crop, and he had parked the tractors in the woods behind our house for a few days, my friend was about a year older than me and he done the plowing with the tractor. When he come back to finish the work the tractor would not start, so he hooked the other tractor to the one that wouldn't start and asked me to pull it off to get it started, I proceeded to try and pull it off but in the meantime the plow was still lowered in the ground and as I tried to pull all the weight my tractor started to rear up from the front, and me looking back I didn't realize it until it was standing on the rear wheels and almost ready to turn over backwards when he pointed at it and I mashed the clutch, and the front wheels fell back down and bounced back up a foot or more before settling down. From then own I never pulled anything without keeping an eye on the front end of the machine I was pulling with. We would use the B Alice chamber to drive to the store and naturally a tractor would not go very fast, so I figured out how to tie the govners open so it would run faster, it would run about 25 miles per hour. We were all very lucky to have the Lord taking care of us or we would have been dead long ago.

About a year or so later my friend's father had a heart attack and died and after he died my friend would drive his father's pickup to school and was as wild as he could be with that truck. A little later his mother traded for a new GMC pickup in which he drove all the time. We went to places together and dated together, where you saw one of us the other weren't far away. He was bad to drink beer and would drive that truck as fast as it would go. I remember it would run past 80 miles per hour, and in 1954 that was very fast for a truck. But thank God we managed to survive and finely his mother got rid of that truck.

In the winter we would take corn to Woodward mill, in Angles' SC, about ten miles away, to get corn ground into meal for corn bread. This was a water driven mill where water from a pond would pass through a water wheel to drive a large round rock with another at its back that ground the corn as it passed between the rocks. When the operator would pour the corn in the cute above the rocks he would use a dipper to scoop out some corn and dumped it in a wooden box on the side, to pay for the grinding cost, this was called toll, so it didn't cost anything for grinding except the toll. We would use one hundred lb white flour sacks to catch the meal as it come out of the mill. This meal was used to make corn bread for the next year.

We would buy flour for our regular bread in one hundred lb sacks, the sacks would have deferent print designs., my aunt Lara would use these flour sacks to make her dresses and bed sheets, this was cheaper and looked as good as bought cloth.

When we gathered our cotton in the late summer, everyone had a burlap cotton sack with a strap sawn on it so you could hang the sack over your shoulder to put the cotton you picked in. If you hired someone to pick cotton you would pay them around two dollars a hundred lb, and all cotton were emptied on a burlap sheet consisting of four two hundred lb fertilizer sacks sowed together, this sheet would hold about two hundred lb of cotton, when tied up, each person's sheet were kept separate, at the end of day you would have your cotton weighed with cotton scales in the field, each person would be paid according to the cotton they picked.

It would take about twelve hundred lb of cotton picked from the field to make a five hundred lb bale after it was ginned. We would haul this twelve hundred lb of cotton about six miles to Jefferson SC where the nearest gin was located.

I remember the large vacuum hose that was used to suck the cotton out of the truck and into the gen. it had a lot of suction to lift the cotton and I would stick my head under it and it would lift my hair straight up and try to pull me in the hose, and one of the gen operators stopped me saying it would take my breath. The hose was about 10 inches. When you are that young you don't see danger the way you do when you are older.

The cotton was ginned, pressed, and baled. The gen owner would generally take the cotton seed for pay except for enough seed to plant next season.

After the cotton was baled my uncle Mack would cut open a small place on the side of the bale to get a sample to take to cotton buyers To find which buyer would pay the most per pound for the cotton.

All bales were numbered and the samples had a matching number, they was several buyers in town and he would go from one to the other until he found the highest bidder, it might be only a quarter to half cent per pound deference, but having a 500 hundred pound bale it would add up. We might make five or six bales per year. One problem we had in September when we would have what we called the September gales, what we know today as hurricanes, if the cotton was not picked before the gales started you could lose most of your crop.

As I got older my uncle told me that I could have what cotton that grew on a 1 acre piece of land to use as I wanted. Good land would produce about a bale of cotton per acre. This was something I enjoyed and looked forward to and had planned on buying an older car with the money. When we gathered it in the fall it made a small bale, about 400 pound. When it was sold I used the money to buy my first car, a 48 mercury convertible, although it had a bad top it was mine and I enjoyed it, but I had to drive it with without license because I wasn't old enough to get my licenses.

When the corn finished growing and the corn filled out we would pull fodder for feed for the mules or horses through the winter, to pull fodder the blades would have to be green and you used both hands to start at the top of the stalk and pull the blades off all the way to the bottom of the stalk, and continue until you got both hands full, using two or three blades you would tie both hand fulls together, break a stalk over and hang the fodder on the stalk to dry. After drying about three days you would go through the rows and tie the fodder in bundles using four small bundles hanging on the stalks for each bundle of fodder, this had to be done in late evening after the dew had accumulated on the fodder to keep it from being brittle, so you could tie it. It would then be hauled to the barn and stored for feed. We would then have to go back later when the corn dried well and pull it and store it in the bar. There was always plenty of work on a farm.

I can remember when we would have eight or ten acres of watermelons, and when they got ripe in early summer, my uncle would have a watermelon buyer to come and walk over the field and give him a price for all the melons that he wanted, he would only won't the ones that weighed 28lb or over and, if he bought them he would bring his crew in and pick all the melons that weighed that or over, and load them on a tractor trailer truck to take them north to sell, and he would leave all of the smaller melons, When he got all he wanted the rest left were ours to do with as we wanted. We would always have more to sell or use as we saw fit, most of the smaller melons we picked and fed to the hogs. For me there were no better tasting watermelon then one busted and eaten in the field, they were something about eating a watermelon outside that made it taste better, or at least I though it did.

Another time I had something to happen, I was about ten years old we were pecking cotton and my uncle Mack had his pickup parked at the field when we saw a fire blazing up in the back of the truck, we run up and put the fire out, it was cotton on fire that was left in the bed. He got mad and accused me of setting the fire playing with matches. I knew I didn't do it but there were no answer why it started, so I started investigating to find out what started it. We always carried a half gallon jar of drinking water with us to the fields, I noticed this jar setting in the sun and saw what had happened, the water in the glass jar had created a magnifying glass when the sun shined through it was in the right spot to heat the cotton hot enough to cause a combustion of the cotton and it would flame up. When I told him I had found what caused the fire he didn't believe me, so I told him I would show him and got a small piece of cotton and the jar of water and placed it where the sun hit the jar in the right place and few minutes later the cotton flamed up. From that day on I have been interested in solar energy.

The black family that lived in the rental house would always plant an acre or more of okra, they would cut it every 2 days when it started bearing, some of my uncles and myself would help them cut the okra when they would get behind, you always had to cut it on time or it would get hard and also stop bearing, an acre of okra is a lot of okra. They would pay us according to how long we worked. They would take the okra to a market and sell it. You always had to make money any way you could to be able to buy the thing you needed.

We all had to do our share to keep things going. On rainy days I would go hunting with a 22 rifle or a 12 ga. Shotgun, a rabbet or squrral was always a treat for next day dinner. I remember one cold morning I were crossing the creek where a tree had fell across making a bridge, caring my 12ga shotgun I saw a squirrel over head on tree limbs, I quickly raised the gun and shot at the squirrel, not only did I miss the squirrel but the gun kicked so hard, and me weighing only about 105 pound, I was knocked off the tree log and into the creek, needless to say I went home wet and cold with no squirrel.

Fishing in black creek was always fun and any fish caught was always good eating, we mostly lived off the land, it was a good life because I guess we didn't know any better.

As I got older I become more and more interested in anything mechanical or electrical, always needing to know what made things work and how to fix things that didn't work anymore, and some things that worked fine but I needed to know what made them work which sometime got me in trouble like taking my aunts sewing machine apart when it was working good, I didn't do that anymore!

When I found several rolls of 16mm film in the trunk of an old junked car in a junkyard where my uncle Ted worked, I thought I hit the jackpot, only problem was there were no projector in the old car, so I could only hold the film up toward light and see one frame at a time which were really too small to tell much about what the subject was. After looking at several frames I thought they all looked alike until I noticed they were a slight deference and figured out if you moved the frames pass light in a motion the figures would change creating a movie effect. So I decided to make my own projector. With an old tin coffee can, a six volt head light bulb, a magnifing glass from an old camera, an old six volt car battery and cutting parts with scissors from tin cans. A car heater motor to drive the shutter and film reel from one of the films, and a white pillow case hung over the back of a chair for a screen, and with everything adjusted I was able to watch the film, they were old westerns but they had no sound. Again my aunt was upset at me for using her good pair of scissors to cut tin cans!

When I were about ten years old I went with my uncle Mack and aunt Lara to McCray's country grocery store near Charlotte NC where I saw a bicycle hanging overhead, the prettiest I thought I had ever seen, I commented about it to my great uncle Mack, he didn't say much about it, but a few days before Christmas that same bicycle showed up at my house. It was a twenty six inch Schwann with wide balloon tires with straight thread on them. Not only was I proud of it, but I were the envy of my friends at school.

Most of my friends had bicycles and we would go to the school and race them around the school house after school, on the back side were a steep hill coming around the corner, on one day I had gained the lead with my bike and started down the hill around the corner of the school house when the bike started to slide, I saw I was going to hit the school house and held my left hand out to stop me from hitting the building, when my hand hit the building I was knocked off the bike, and when I got up I had a terrible pain in my left wrist, I wouldn't tell anybody when I got home and my arm hurt so bad I could hardly stand it, but never went to a doctor, and it really hurt for several days. About 2 years later my uncle Mack had to go to the doctor for his foot that he thought he had broke, at that time doctors had what were called fluoroscopes that they could put your foot under it and see the bones of your foot, it was made to fit shoes, I had gone with him to the doctor and went in the office with him and saw what the doctor done with the fluoroscope, when he was through I asked if I could look at my arm to see if I had broken it earlier, he let me put my arm under the fluoroscope. He saw, and pointed out to me where my arm had been fractured earlier; you could see the old fracture that had healed. The fluoroscopes were later outlawed due to radiation. That was the first time my uncle Mack knew about me hitting the school house with my bike. Back then you didn't go to a doctor unless it was something real bad, like life threatening or pain so bad you could hardly stand it.

As I got older, about 13 years old I started working on bicycles at a garage where my uncle Ted worked on automobiles, he worked for a couple who owned a parts store on the top floor over the garage, I would replace wheel bearings and align rims by adjusting the spokes which was very difficult until you learned how to adjust them in the right direction to pull the wheel straight. About 6 month later my uncle left the garage to work for the ladies husband who had bought a junk yard at a different location. The lady asked me if I would like to run the shop and install parts that she sold in the parts store to customers, which she now owned. I happily said that I would love to; I was 14 years old at the time.

For the next year or more I worked on automobiles and installed parts that the parts store sold to customers. just an idea of what my rates were, I charged one dollar to change a starter or a generator, adjust brakes for one dollar per wheel, install brake shoes for three dollars per wheel, this is to give an idea of what my labor charge was, not bad when a laborer made around three dollars a day on the farm. But the main thing was I had some money to spend and enjoyed what I was doing, and made a lot of friends while working there. Back in those days there was no problem with child labor as it is today, there were no questions about your age.

I would also work on peoples cars and trucks at home in the back yard under a tree, that why some people called me a shade tree mechanic. These folks would learn about me from hearing about me running the shop in Pageland and would come to my house, I would always try to help them and fix anything they had that I could fix, I remember when a farmer drove his Farmall tractor up in the yard late one evening and it sounded like the whole motor was about to fall out, the connecting rods were knocking so bad it sound like they were going to come out the side of the block, He asked me if I could fix it, and I told him it sounded so bad I didn't know whether it was beyond repair or not, he wanted me to tear it down and see if I could repair it. I pulled the bottom pan down and found all the connecting rod bearings were wore out but hadn't damaged the crankshaft, so I got all the parts I needed and rebuilt the motor, when I finished and started it up it sounded like a new motor. I went by his house and left word that his tractor was ready, we had no phones in those days, he later come to get the tractor and could not believe it run so good, he said it didn't run that good when it was new. From that job on he would tell everyone to come to me to get things fixed and I stayed busier than I wanted to be, but I enjoyed that type work.

Another time a friend come driving up on a bulldozer and parked it on the side of the road, come to the house and asked for me, when I come out he said he had a bad clutch in his dozer an wanted to know if I could put a new one in for him, I had never seen a clutch in a caterpillar before and didn't know where to start and told him so, he said I could find out how to do it because he didn't know anybody else that would replace it. I agreed to tear it down and replace it if he would buy the clutch, I knew somebody had built it and at least I could find a way to repair it, I continued to take the clutch out and found it was not as bad as I thought it would be, the only bad part was it being so heavy, after finding the right tools I replaced it and it worked out good, and I got to drive it around and check it out. I always loved bulldozers, and I had got to work on one and it worked great. When the man come to get it he drove it around the yard, come back and paid me and gave me a tip. I never charged as much as I should but I enjoyed working on this kind of things.

On weekends me and some of my friends would get together, some of them had old cars, and we would drive the county back roads looking for ways to have some fun, the roads were dirt and dusty, no one had drivers license and everybody, including the deputy sheriff knew each other and knew we had no license, the deputy would spot us turn on his red light {that were before they went to blue lights} being at night and dusty roads we would have several mile chase until we would decide to lose the deputy, we would turn off our lights, turn on a side road, when the deputy would pass we would go back the other way and go home and park behind our house. At that time there was only two deputies to cover that part the county. When I got older I realized how dangerous and dumb this was, although I think the deputy enjoyed it as much as we did.

One of the funniest things I think I ever saw was at a pond close to our home. There was a family that lived only about a quarter mile from us, and there were two young men that was several years older than me, the youngest had been in the mental hospital in Columbia SC for several years, but had got out and come home. We become good friends and would go places together, so we went fishing at this pond. The older brother owned a 1929 model A ford coupe with a rumble seat in the back. He drove the car to the pond and we started fishing, a little later the other brother quit fishing an told his brother he was going to clean the carburetor on the car. His brother and myself keep on fishing but I could see the car from where I was, I noticed he would keep trying to start the car using a hand crank he would turn the crank for a while and stop and wipe his face, finely I noticed him pushing the car toward a small hill, and as I watched he started toward the downhill slope, he had pulled the throttle on the steering wheel to wide open passion, and was running along beside the car, and reached in with his right hand and slapped the transmission shifter in second gear, with the clutch being engaged, and the throttle wide open with the car in gear it started and was running at a high rate of speed, he was holding to the steering wheel with his right hand and the door frame with his left hand, and his feet were starched straight out behind him, he went out of sight going up the road and around a curve in that passion. While I was trying to get the attention of his brother, I heard the car coming back. He had somehow managed to get in the seat, got control, turned the car around and come back down the road wide open. After it was over I thought it was the funniest thing I had ever seen. Thankfully it didn't turn into a disaster.

This same friend of mine was plowing one day when the mule pulling the plow would not turn at the end of the row, he would almost have to drag him around, this happened several times and he kelp getting angry and angrier so he stopped and walked up to the front of the mule and slapped the mule in the side of the head as hard as he could, which really didn't hurt the mule, but after he had hit him and plowed another few rows he started feeling sorry for slapping the mule, there was an apple tree in the field loaded with green apples, so he pulled up under the tree stopped the mule and pulled off an apple and handed it to the mule, and the mule reached and grabbed the apple and one of his fingers and almost bit it off, he said he guessed the mule was just getting even with him for slapping his head.

One day I was visiting a friend when his father come in the room, knowing how much I liked to make things work, he offered to show me a set of drawings where he had designed of a flame thrower that he said his son in law used in world war two. He said he designed the device and gave the drawings to defense department to be developed and used in the war, and told me how successful it had been. I asked him if he got any money for it and he said anything you made during war would be taken for defense and the government would not be responsible to pay for it. He would not tell me what type of energy he used, saying he was a sworn to secret.

My grandfather always loved to fox hunt, and had seven or eight fox hounds and every Saturday night he would go out in the sand hills and turn the dogs loose, they would go deferent ways until one would pick up a fox trail and you could hear him let out a long hollering howl and start trailing letting out a trailing howls and all other dogs would join him and the race were on, you could hear them for two or three miles away, and he loved the music the dogs made, he could tell the voice of each dogs bark and tell you the dogs name. I would sometimes go with him and my uncles but I was never very interested in hearing dogs run a fox. They would sometime run to well after midnight and they would then have to get all the dogs back before they could go home, and that were always hard to do. He had a cow horn he would blow and most of the time the dogs would come to the sound of the horn, but sometimes it would be the next day before he would get all the dogs back home, but he would do the same thing again the next Saturday night, he loved listening to the dogs run that good.

On Sundays after dinner my uncles would get together in the back yard and practice fighting, they would pull off their shirts and fight as hard as they could, the only rules was not to hit each other in the face or head. My grandfather had a leather strap and if any of the boys got out of order he would get hold of them and they wouldn't do what they were doing anymore, he believed in discipline and to have respect for each other. It was common for one to get cracked ribs and have to work hurting for several days. But they would never get mad at each other. I guess that's why they liked to fight in bars so much. I guess it was good I wasn't big or heavy enough to fight like that, or I might have been in trouble like most of them always got in at bars. I didn't think that was the best way to have fun anyway.

When I was growing up I had seven uncles on my mother's side of the family, four was from one to six years older than me, and I had four aunts. I never knew many relatives on my father's side of the family. I had nine half brothers and sisters that I never was very close to because I was never around them; it was only later in life that I got to know them and my biological father as well. My uncles on my mother's side were the guys I was always around and went to places with, which was not always good. They were all bad to drink beer and get in fights.

On Saturday nights, we would get together and go to Pageland to a café on main street where they would all drink beer and get high, the place was always full of people and all of them would be drinking, I was never a guy to drink very much, but they would get in trouble and loved a good fist fight, if no one started a fight, two of my uncles would be setting in a booth and all of a sudden one would hit the other and he would fall out of the booth soon the whole room would be fighting, this would go on until the police would show up and start asking questions and we would sneak out the rear door and leave. This would happen almost every Saturday night. This keep on until it got where other groups would come in from another part of the county, and then we would have a rival group. The main group was the Mt. Crogan guys, we never got along. One Saturday night my uncle Casey went to the bath room and I saw two of the Mt crogan guys follow him in, I knew he was in trouble, before I could tell the rest of my uncles, I saw this big man come running out of the bath room holding his stomach and the other following behind him, I knew something was wrong, so we all left out the back door before the police arrived, the next week we heard that the guy had to have a lot of stitches in his stomach, when we asked Casey what happened, he said one of the men said "we got you now", that's when he pulled out his pocket knife and walked around the guy cutting him. We never heard any more about this.

Another time we were at the café on Saturday night and the Mount Crogan gang was running their mouth about us and left the café, we flowered them on the way back to Mt. Crogan, outside of Pageland on hwy 9 there's a curve called the dead man's curve, my uncle Hargett had a 1949 mercury and they were driving an old model chevarlot sedan, when we approached that dead man's curve I were in the back seat and could see the speedometer at over 100 miles per hour, we passed their car and was meeting a tractor trailer truck at the same time, I thought everything were over and closed my eyes. But somehow we missed the truck and car. Another time God spared my life.

My uncle Casey was the worst one to fight, there was a guy named Harry Laney that lived in Pageland and always visited the café on main street where they sold beer, and Casey went there also, the two looked so much alike you would think they were twin brothers, and hated each other so much they would fight every time they meet, they didn't need a reason. One night they were in the café and started fighting and the police was called, while they were breaking up the fight Casey said he wasn't going to jail and ran out the front door and across the street, one of the police pulled his gun and shot at him and hit the brick building beside him as he keep running, for several years afterwards you could see the chip knocked out of a brick where the bullet hit. He continued to hide until the next day when he and his brother left and went to Massutous, and didn't return for about a year, when he decided to return home, he stopped in Pageland and went in the police department, and told them who he was and he wanted pay his fine, to everyone's surprise they took his money for the fine and let him go.

When I got old enough to get my drivers license, I went to Pageland police department where a state patrol would come one day a week to give driver license test. When I passed the written part I come back the next week for the driver's test, I were using one of my friends cars to take the test, when the patrolman got in the car he gave me the directions to go, so I proceeded to go the route he told me to, which were to the red light and turn right and go one block and turn left, when I started out I went to the light, gave my right hand signal and proceeded to go one block, give a left hand signal and began to turn left when a car behind me started blowing his horn, I proceeded to turn as I had signaled, when the patrolman asked me did I see that car, I never answered the officer, knowing I was making a legal turn. We went on and I parlled parked and then returned to the police dept. I didn't know what to think after I didn't answer him when asked me the question, but when we got out and started in the station he said I'm going to issue you your licensed. I still don't know why he asked me if I saw that car.

Back in the mid 1950's in South Carolina you didn't need a birth certificate or a drivers permit to learn to drive, you only had to fill out an application take a written test and road test and if you passed both they would issue your license,.

I had just got my drivers license when my uncle Hargett decided to go to Florida for a week or so and asked me to go with him. He had bought a 1946 cheverlot coupe at Marks auto shop in Fort Mill SC, We only had a few dollars together but we started to Florida, we would drive until we got tired and would stop and sleep a few hrs and go again. I remember We stopped beside the road somewhere close to Leesburg Fla., we saw what we thought was an orange grove we had never seen oranges growing before, the trees were hanging full of the biggest oranges I had ever seen. There was no traffic on the road, so we walked in the grove and picked some oranges, we ate several, and they were the best and sweetest oranges I had ever had. We still had some left so we put them in the back seat of the car, about two days later we decided to eat some more of the oranges, but to our surprise they was all grape fruit and tasted nothing like oranges we had picked grape fruit all along, I guess we were so hungry we thought they were sweet.

We continued to go further south where farming increased with all kind of vegetables and a lot of migrant workers mostly from Puerto Rico. We had no problem finding food with all the produce available, you could eat all you wanted without paying anything for it, the only expense we had was our gas for the car, and gas were only about 20 to 25 cents per gallon at that time, we would sleep in the car and if we needed some more money we could meet a truck in the morning and go out with the migrant workers to gather produce in the fields, you were only required to give your name and you would get paid at the end of the day, and they always paid in cash, whatever you were picking you were paid by the basket full, All we needed was a little money for gas anyway. We stayed about a week before starting back home. It was an experience I'll never forget but I wouldn't want to do it again.

That same year my uncle John, who lived in Pontiac Mich. And worked for Pontiac Motors. He wanted to move back to South Carolina and asked me if I would go with him to Mich. And drive one of his cars back and pull a trailer with a load of his stuff, I agreed and when we got there we had to put a transmission in a 1949 Buick Road master straight eight, that was the car I was to use to pull a trailer back to South Carolina, it was cold with about six inches of snow on the ground and we only had a shed to get under to change the transmission. When we finished I remember pulling that trailer loaded back home. When we come through Columbus Ohio, that had the most red lights I had ever seen, the instructions he gave me was when I got in Columbus to drive the speed limit and not go slower or faster at any time because the lights were timed so I would not have to stop for red lights and I did and it worked, but the scary part was when I got in the mountains pulling a loaded trailer on the mountain curves, that were before we had interstate highways. That was another experience I will never forget. Again the man upstairs took care of me and I arrived back in South Carolina safe.

After leaving the auto shop job I went to work for my uncle Ted who at that time owned a junk yard, who offered me twenty dollars a week to take parts off old cars and help sell them to customers. This wasn't as much as I was making, but it wasn't as hard and, I had more free time to work on other projects at home.

When I was about seventeen years old a neighbor, Hubert king stopped by my house and asked if I would look at his car and see if I could fix it, He lived about a half mile away and had lived there only a short time. I agreed and went to his house to check his car and when I arrived I noticed a buiteful girl carrying a bucket from the barn to the house, and I asked who she was, knowing he wasn't marred so it wouldn't be his wife, he said it was his sister. A few days later I was passing the house and saw her in the yard, I stopped and spoke to her and asked her name and if she were marred. She said her name was Kathleen, and no she wasn't marred. I asked her for a date and she said she wasn't allowed to date anyone, but I could visit any time.

Several days later I got the courage to visit to ask her brother Hubert how his car was doing. In the meantime she had asked if she could date me, and was told that I could come to see her but we couldn't go anywhere, we would have to stay in the house and visit. She was a little over seventeen years old at the time. I learned later that her father had died several years earlier and her brother Hubert didn't won't her to get marred because he wanted her to stay home and work in the fields and take care of the animals. Her brother Hubert was known to have an awful temper and always wanted everything his way or he would get valiant. We dated for the next year and never went anywhere alone. During that time we fell more deeply in love and started planning our future together. When we decided to get marred we didn't let anyone know except her mother who lived their also. She was one of the nicest ladies I have ever known. She asked us to leave when Hubert was gone so there wouldn't be any trouble. In the meantime we had slipped all her clothes out of the house and took them to my house, I proceeded to get our marriage linicene and on March 14th 1959 late in the evening when her brother Hubert was gone somewhere, I laid my shotgun in the floor of the car and along with her nephew Bo who insisted on coming with me to pick her up. He really didn't like Hubert and was a good friend of mine, He was known as someone who would fight for any one he liked. And he always seemed to like me. I pulled up in the yard in a 1949 Ford owned by my uncle Ted, she got in the car and we left to get married by the probate judge in Lancaster SC. after I dropped Bo off in Pageland. And continued on to Lancaster and to the probate judge's office.

After we got marred we come back to Pageland where my uncle Ted and his wife lived and spent our first night with them. The following Monday we moved all our belongings to a small trailer at Uncle Ted's junk yard that he rented us for ten dollars a month. where we lived for the next few months.

My wife loved her mother vary much but was afraid to go back to see her because of her brother Hubert. In about three weeks after we were marred I got a massage from her brother Hubert that he had trouble with the starter on his car, and wanted me to check it. I didn't know whether he really had problems with his car, or was tricking me to come back to his house, knowing how sneaky he could be, but my wife wanted to see her mother so bad I decided that we would go and see if he really had problem with the starter. Thankfully he did have starter problems and I repaired it and we always got along good from that time on.

When we got marred I had twenty dollars left after I paid the probate Judge Five dollars for marring us. We lived on the twenty dollars a week I made at the junk yard before I paid the ten dollar rent and bought groceries until I got my next job at The Springs Cotton Mills in Fort Mill SC November, 1st 1959.

After working at the junk yard for several months for twenty dollars per week, I decided that I needed to make more money to have the things we wanted in life. I had a friend that worked in Fort mill SC at Springs Cotton Mills, He told me I needed to apply for a job there. About a week later I traveled to Fort Mill and put in an application at the personnel office and give the friends name that would contact me at the junk yard. We had no telephones at that time. A week later I got word that the personnel department wanted to interview me. I went for my interview and the personnel manager called Brice Douglas who was the air condition overseer to interview me, after talking with him he hired me. My pay was $1.15 per hour and we worked 48 hours a week plus 8 hours every other Sunday, with all over 40 hours per week we were paid time and half. Vary good money according to what I was making before.

The first day of work I was introduced to my coworkers and was told what I was to do. We went to work at 6am and worked until 2pm, we all met in the shop at 6 o'clock and about 6:30 we would go to the cafeteria for breakfast. I asked one of my coworkers when we were going to work, he said we always went to breakfast or to get coffee before we started. After about 7:00am we would go on to our assigned job and start working. About every half hour we would take a break for at least 15 minutes. At 11:30 we went back to the cafeteria for lunch. Growing up on a farm and working the way we had to I could not believe we worked so little. A lot of my coworkers would complain about having to work so hard, I felt like I was on a vacation with pay. My job were very dirty with the classification of air condition cleaner, whitch consisted of cleaning air handling equipment. I was assigned about 20 air ducts in the weaving department with the room tempeture of being around 86 degrees and around 85% humidity. These ducts would sweat and get completely wet, with all the lint in the air, it would all settle on the wet ducts causing slim and a nasty mess. I would have to keep these ducts wiped off with yarn waste and a bucket with water in it, to put the waste in. At the end of day my clothe would be filthy. The work wasn't hard but very dirty.

From the time I went to work at Springs until the late sixty's when the OHSA laws went into effect some of the conditions we worked in were bad, from dusty and noisy situations to unhealthy and dangerous situations, on Sundays when the plant was shut down, we would clean out copper air ducts by crawling through the ducts with an air hose and blowing out the dry lint that were stuck inside, when we would exit the duct we would cough up green copper dust for hours, we would wear mask while we were inside the ducts but that didn't stop all the dust, We also would use a hack saw to cut and remove asbestos insulation on steam pipes that needed repair, these things was never a concern at that time.

When OHSA became law the company went from no regulations to extreme regulations. I think all supervision went from not thinking a lot about hardus things to being afraid that OHSA would do an inspection and fine the company, and the supervisor would lose their job. Different departments would be stricter then others, all air condition employees were required to wear hard hats all the time they were inside the plant, with no one else in the plant required to wear them. This caused a lot of complaints from the employees. We were also required to wear hearing protection and eye protection. Other departments didn't do. This caused a lot of resentments by employees. In our department, later on these rules were relaxed to what was safe and what protected our health.

In the mid 1960's I had an experience I hope I never have again, I was making my rounds checking the air condition on my job at Springs Mills Fort Mill Plant when I saw some smoke coming from a loom in the weaving department a few ailes over and went to investigate thinking it was a fire from the loom, to my shock I saw this loom fixer slumped over the loom and white smoke coming up where he was touching the loom, knowing what I knew about electricity I knew what had happened and got the supervisor to turn off the power, unforuthly it was too late. For months after that I would see that scene any time I closed my eyes, I knew this guy and was friends with him and could only think of his wife and children and what they were going through.

From my early childhood, I had a friend that I went to school with and after we quit school, we were always together, went on dates together, went fishing together, and was always very close, like brothers. He went to work at Springs Mills before I did but when I come to fort mill we would get together again on occasions and go fishing in the river, but we were both married then and had our family's to occupy our time but he still would go fishing with another friend with a boat. At that time I was a member of the Fort Mill Rescue squad. Late one evening I got a call that we had a drowning on the Catawba River so I went to the squad station and found out it was my childhood friend and his fishing buddy was both missing and they had found there boat. I proceeded to go with the squad to the river and helped drag for the bodies and after several hours we found one, and a little later we found the other. Being as close as we had been from our childhood it was very hard for me to go through this ordeal. Knowing him from childhood I knew he couldn't swim, but for some reason neither were wearing a life Jacket. The rest of the squad members didn't know how close we had been and I didn't say anything about it to them, which I guess made it worse on me.

When I told uncle Ted that I had another job, he got very angry and told me not to go back to his trailer to get anything out of the trailer, not even our clothes, but I went anyway and got our clothes, we stayed at my uncle Mack's until we moved to Fort Mill.

For the next month I would meet a station wagon in the morning at 4:45 AM that cared riders from that area to Fort Mill and back in the evening for five dollars a week. I had to meet the ride half way between Pageland and Monroe at five in the morning, leave my car in a store parking lot until that evening. At that time we worked from six o'clock in the morning until two o'clock in the evening. It would take me an hour to get to work and an hour to get home.

Times were hard in those days, but if you worked hard and used your money wisely, and bought only the things that were absolute necessary you would find a way to make ends meet.

When we moved to Fort Mill about four weeks after I got the job, I rented a two room apartment from Mr. Mark's on Spratt Street where we lived for several months. My wife didn't work but Mr. Mark asked if she would like to do some house work and help take care of his dad who couldn't get around very well. This would help pay the rent, and she did, we later moved to Link Street to a bigger three room apartment. Later that year my boss, Brice Douglas had a brick apartment on Morgan Street that he rented, when it come open, he asked if I would like to rent it, being a much nicer place, I rented it. At that time my wife Kat was pregnant with our first child.

We were living on Morgan Street when our first child was born at York General Hospital in Rock Hill SC, on June twenty sixth nineteen sixty. It was a boy and we named him Ricky Carson.

After living there for a few months he sold the apartment to a family that planed to move in it later, and when he got ready to move in he give me a month to find another house, so they could move in this one. I found another house on 105 Sumner Street that I rented from Max Hinson who owned Ford motor co. in Fort Mill. When we moved in, Kat was pregnant with our second child. We lived there until we bought the house where we live now. On January 2nd 1962 I was called from work to tell me her water had broke, I went home and carried her to the hospital and our second child was born before I could get her signed in a room, that was cutting it close, it was another boy, we named him Robby Wayne. In the meantime I was looking at a house off what is now Barberville road, I paid the man 200.00 dollars and took up the payments, and bought the house with 1 acre land, when Robby was about six weeks old and Ricky was 18 month older we moved in our new house. The house was built by Jim Waters Homes and was not finished on the inside, we had no well and no bathroom but we owned a home. For the next several months we had it hard, carrying water, using an outside toilet and finely getting a well drilled, and working on the inside of the house. And I was working at my job six days a week and every other Sunday. It was hard on all of us, but we were determent to make it work and after a lot of hard work and by the grace of God we finely got our home where we could live comfortable and I have lived here now for over 50 years.

I was always making something even if it were toys with no benefit except the satisfaction of building it. In the early 1960's I decided to build a flying saucer, a toy of course, I got some polyethylene like we used on wood floors in the plant and some cloth for backing, and made a mold with wire the shape I wanted the flying saucer to look like and when I got it shaped the way I wanted I wet the cloth with the polyurethane and laid the cloth over the wire frame and smoothed it out to dry, I then made the dome with several round port holes cut out, and made it look like what I had seen on TV, of course my two sons was always watching and excited, after everything were done and all urethane had got hard I proceeded to paint it with silver paint, some of our friends would pass by and see it setting behind our house and would stop to see what it was. They were always festinated with how real it looked.

After we moved to the country off, what is now Barberville road in the early sixties I bought an old 1937 Chevrolet coupe, I installed a v8 motor in it, had Zack Smith to do some body work and paint it, I always wanted something different so I mounted a small TV in the dash, the TV had a 120 volt power supply, so I opened it up and found where I could change some wires and reduce it down to 12volts, where it would work on the car battery. The TV worked good but I never thought about it being illegal to have a TV in view of the driver until a friend asked if it were legal to drive it with a TV in view, when I checked the law not only was it illegal but it could cause you have an accident,. Sure wish I had that car today.

In the early 1960's I found out that I didn't have a birth certificate in the name I was using, and started checking to find out what I needed to do. When I was born and my birth certificate was recorded it had the name, Wade Donald Anderson and, after my mother died, my father deeded me to my great uncle Maxey Steen, he decided he didn't want me to carry that name so he change it to Carson Donald Steen, but it was never probated so my name were never legal and there was no records of the change. I went to school using the name Carson Donald Steen, When I got my drivers license my uncle Mack signed that I were of age, and when I got our marriage lencese he also signed that I was 18 years old and, my future wife had her birth certificate.

When I went to work at Springs I only had to give them my social security number and tell them my age, and when I got my social security number, I only had to send in my information and it were mailed to me. In the name I gave which was Carson Donald Steen, They never asked for any proof of who I was.

At that time I was married, had two children that had a false name on their birth certificate and social security card and, I had a false name on my driver's license. After talking to a lawyer he recommended that the simplest way was to have my name changed from Wade Donald Anderson to Carson Donald Steen by the order of a Judge. So the Lawyer proceeded to prepare all paper work to get my name changed. After a month or so I got the decree where my name was changed and a birth certificate was issued with the name of Wade Donald Anderson to Carson Donald Steen by court order. This was quite a job to get done but it was worth the time and effort.

I always liked drag racing. So I decided to build a drag rail in the early 1960's, so I got together the parts I needed and started building the chassis, I used an old Chevrolet pickup straight axle for the front axle, the chassis was made with two 20 foot length of 1 3/4 inch schugel 40 pipe, with the front axle mounted on one end and a 1949 ford rear end on the other, with a 49 Ford v8 motor attached to an older model Plymouth three speed transmission with a short driveshaft which consisted of a double universal joint that I fabricated, at that time my uncle Ted and I had buried the hatchet from the earlier times when I left his junk yard for my job at Fort Mill. So I got all the parts I needed from him at no cost if I put Steen's Junk Yard on a panel on the rail, without getting free parts I could not have built the dragster, because supporting a wife and two children left me with no extra money. When I finished the rail some friends and myself carried the dragster to Pageland SC drag strip where we tested it, there were only a few lights at the starting line and as you went down the track it become completely dark, we had no lights on the dragster so I relied on a flashlight in one hand and drove with the other I had fabricated a roll cage out of ¾ inch conduit, the only purpose it served was the appearance, The brakes was an emergency brake pulley on the rear of the transmission with a band around it and a lever to pull to activate it. The track owner had no problems with us running. I had mud grip tires on the back and regular tires on front, the track was dirt and they keep it scraped with a motor grader to keep it smooth. The dragster was so light it would leave the line like it was shot out of a gun. I had made eight straight pipes that replaced the exhaust manifolds about 8 inches long. When I would rive up the motor, fire would stand out of the 4 pipes on each side of the motor, when it was dark the fire would light up the ground around the dragster. At that time they were some guys that owned a new 1963 Plymouth with hemi engines, they were running about 96 mph in the 1/8 mile. When they would leave the starting line it would look like a tornado out of the back with the dust from the wheels and the tires would spin so fast it would take a few seconds for the car to get moving at the speed it was capable of doing. I remember one time I lined up beside one of these hemi powered Plymouth, when the light changed I left the starting line while the guy in the other car was trying to get traction, and was almost half way down the track when he got traction and started moving, so I beat him to the finish line, when we come back the return road to the tower, he keep going and left the track, I went to the tower and got my trophy. I think it embarrassed him to get out run by a flat head Ford motor and a homemade rail. The things I did in those days, I could only have done, and lived to tell about it if not for the Lord taking care of me.

Back in the early to late 1960's I was an avid nascar fan and went to a lot of races, I remember going to a Bristol race about four hours away with two friends from work. I had just bought a 1963 Ford fast back and I drove it, I always enjoyed driving in the mauntains and screeching the tires around all curves, the guy on the passenger side reached outside the door and with his fist hit the side of the door, it sound like a rock had hit it when I looked at him and I asked what was that, he asked if I didn't see that mail box that his elbow hit. We were always pulling tricks on each other. That were fun days but we did crazy things.

I had been working for Springs for about four years, had two children and my wife to support and being the only one bringing home a check was hard to make ends meet. My wife knew how hard it was and wanted to go to work to help. She put in an application at the personal department at Springs and was interviewed and given a test, but she was never called or told why she wasn't hired, after several weeks, knowing they had hired several people after she had applied I started asking questions and found out that she hadn't made a good enough score on the test they gave her, growing up on a farm she had never been around or associated with the kind of questions the test asked, she was just a common country girl without a high school education but she was a person that knew what hard work was like and didn't mind doing it. That was before the test was eliminated due to not being fair. I was talking one day to a supervisor in the spooling department about it, and he said he had an opening in his department and needed an employee to fill the job and would be glad to take her and train her for that job. He talked to his boss and they agreed to hire her. His supervisor went to the personnel department and insisted they hire her. She worked for 24 years at Springs and made an outstanding employee without one blemish on her record. She was one of the hardest working people I ever knew, and was told the same by her coworkers many times. That was the way she was brought up and helped teach our two sons the same work esthetes. I was always so proud of her and loved her so much.

In the early 1960's I was at a service station on white street, that were owned by an older gentleman that also had a heating oil service and a radiator repair shop. A month or so before the man who repaired radiators had died. I had become good friends with the owner, and one day while I was in his place of business, he asked me if I would like to operate the radiator shop in the evenings after I got off work at the mill, he said he would show me everything he knew about radiator repair and would give me a month free rent to get started. At that time we had two small children and I was the only one working, so after talking to my wife I decided to give it a try. I repaired radiators after work for the next two years or longer until the gentleman that owned the business died. I learned a lot about repairing radiators, replacing cores and repairing leaks, and testing for leaks. One day a man come in with a gas tank he had removed from his car, he said it had a bad leak, and wanted me to repair it, as we was talking the owner of the shop happened to walk up and asked what was I doing with that gas tank, I said I was going to repair it, as I was cleaning off all the dirt so I could solder it, he started cursing and said I was going to blow up the whole building, and I assured him it would be safe, but I don't think he believed me, he walked around to the other side of the building outside. I filled the gas tank with water up to the place I were going to solder, and continued to fix the hole, and called them and said I had finished. He would tell people that come in after that I was crazy, but I knew what I was doing. No gas fumes, no explosion, and the water had removed all the fumes.

I can remember when President Kennedy was shot and where I was, we were listing to a radio in the shop at Springs Fort Mill Plant on Friday November 22nd 1963 when it was announced on the radio that were playing in the leather shop that the President had been shot in Dallas Texas, everybody stopped working and went to the leather shop to listen to the radio to hear what the details were, and after a few hours it were confirmed the President was dead, everybody were in shock some with tears some shaking their heads, it didn't matter wither you liked him or not, he was our president and it was a sad day in our history. I was watching TV the following Sunday morning when they were moving Lee Harvey Oswell when Jack Ruby come out of the crowd and shot him on live TV. This is a time that I'll never forget.

I remember when Kennedy he said we would go to the moon by the end of the decade and was listening to the radio in my car inside the company fence while I was waiting for my wife to get off work when the news broke saying the Eagle had landed, those words would make goose bumps rise all over your body. The President's Promises had been kelp.

I had worked for Springs for about two years when one afternoon I found out my boss had once again placed a guy on a mechanic's job that had only been hired a few month, this was the second time in a year I had been passed over, and I knew I was better qualified then this guy, so I come in early the next morning and met my boss at the back gate and asked him why I had been passed over the second time, at that time the company had no rules that required the posting of any job when it come open or when a new job was created, he said he had to put who he thought was best qualified on the job, I asked him to tell me why this guy were better qualified then me, when I had worked for him over a year longer, he couldn't answer my question, so I proceeded to tell him that I had no intentions to work the rest of my life as an air condition cleaner, and if he wasn't satisfied with my work I was ready to leave now, he said I was doing a good job but my education was not as good as it should be, I told him all I ever wanted was a chance to prove what I could do. One of my coworkers was present when we were talking, and he spoke up and started complaining why he was passed over, that's when my boss looked him straight in the eye and said, you can say too much, and that was when the coworker turned and walked away.

About two month later my boss come to me and said the shop superentdent wanted to talk to me, so I went in his office and he asked me to have a seat. He then asked me if I would like to work for him while one of his employees went to National Guard training for six months. He had two employees that worked the entire plant repairing lights, replacing bulbs, and cleaning lint out of electric motors in the spinning department. He said I would make more per hour but I would get only forty hours per week, I agreed to take the job, because I already worked at a radiator shop in the evenings. For the next six month I worked with my coworker a learned a lot about electricity and how to repair florescent lights. Some days we would replace 75 or more florescent bulbs and replace several ballast in the lights. This was experience that helped me understand how electricity worked and how to work on it safely.

About that time I started attending York Tec and for the next several years I completed a total of nineteen short courses in air condition and electrical, and each coarse were about forty hours long with two hour sessions three times a week, I knew I needed the technical education to be able to communicate with the people I come in contact with on my job.

The instructor that taught most of the curses were Mr. Lacy White one of the best teachers I think I have ever had, he was a very smart man and knew how to get the point across and was interested in you learning. He would always tell his students at the beginning of the course to ask questions, no question is stupid however simple it might be, and if he heard any student laugh at a question someone asked he would remember it and when the time was right he would pin him on the wall before the rest of the class to see.

During this time we also had to check the emergency lights through the plant, they were battery operated and would come on if we had a power failure, one day we were working in the spinning room when a man that worked for the outside engineering department was running a new water line, knowing we worked on emergency lights, he asked if we could move that light to the other side of the post so he could get his line buy, we didn't see any reason we could not and, we always tried to help each other, so we proceeded to move the light. About two days later our boss called us in his office and asked if we moved that emergency light and we said we did and told him why, that's when he went off on both of us, he told us that we were never to move anything if he didn't instruct us to do so, he also said one morning he would come in and one of his air compressors would be gone if he didn't stop people from doing this, (the air compressors weighted about three tons) but he got his point across and we both learned a lesson. A few days later he walked by us in the shop and smiled and asked if we had moved any more emergency lights. We assured him we had learned our lesson.

When the six month was over and the other guy come back, at that time the company had a policy that insured an employee his job back when he got out of service, the shop superintendent went to my prier boss and told him that I had learned a lot in that six month, and he should find me a job back with him. He happened to have an opening, so he give it to me. In about two weeks the second shift mechanic quit to go to Bowater's corp. which left his job open, that was when my boss come to me and said I'm going to put you on this job on the second shift and if you can't run it I will take you off. I stayed on the second shift for the next six years and never had to call help in but one time, and that was a steam line burst and I couldn't find the turnoff valve, and when he got there he couldn't find it either and had to call outside engineering. I had the reasonability of all air condition motors, controls, conditions and anything that pertained to air condition with no helper.

While I was working at springs as an air condition mechanic I was responsible for the temperature and humidity throughout the plant. In the weaving department the humidity had to be around 85% for the looms to run good, any lower the warp yearn would brake and the loom would stop, if it got two high the warp threads would stick together and matt up and the yearn would break. If the weavers though the humidity was too dry or too wet they would raise cane until their supervisor would call me to check the conditions on their job, I would come check the condition on their job and if it was off from where it should be I would fix it, but if it was all right you never told them that it was all right, I learned that very quick I would always tell them I would be back a little later to see how it was doing. When I would come back by usually they would say it was running better. If they got it in their head that it wasn't right then they would lose confidence and it seemed to run vary bad. You could never tell a weaver that nothing was wrong with the condition. But you had to let them know you were on their side and trying to help, and you could do it without lying to them. I got along good with all the weavers in the plant. The spinning department was the same but not as bad. There temperature would run about 85 degrees and 55% which wasn't as critical as the weave room. You always had to do everything you could to make everybody's job run at its best and never lie to them.

One day the plant manager stopped me and said I see you have attended a lot of courses at York Tec and I said yes I feel like I need all the education I can get, He said, I have to sign off on the money you spent for the courses so we could pay you back, at that time if you took courses that pertained to your job the company would pay you back when you successfully completed the course, that's when he asked me if I would like to go to the companies supervisor course and I said I would, so he set things up for me to attend, and told my supervisor the dates and told him to make arrangements to cover my job while I was going, this was a break I got by showing that I wanted to improve my chances to move up in the company and about a year later I was offered a job in supervision, and it was this manger that recommended me. I held this job along with several promotions until I went in my own business.

The personnel manager and I become good friends later on and he told me one day that I were the only department head without a high school education in the whole origination and at that time the company had about eighteen plants in the south east. Back then the company had a mechanical apptude test that would tell how much mechanical ability you had, I took the test but they would not tell anybody what their score was, they would only say you passed or failed, later on they discarded this test due to some kind of government rules, but this same personnel manager told me after I left the company that

I made the highest score that had ever been made. That made me feel good and he even gave me the test questions for keep sake, the questions were common sense and I answered accordingly he said he were told to get rid of the question booklet and he thought I would be the right person to give it to.

When I were working for Springs I saw a need for a device that you could cut a keyway in a shaft without having to remove it from the machine, I designed a device that would clamp around the shaft and by using a milling cutter and a ½ inch drill motor you could rotate the shaft to the other side, from the bad keyway and cut another keyway. This would save several hours of labor, removing the shaft and caring it to the shop to cut it with a milling machine.

I was always trying to make improvements on anything mechanical or electoral, the first car I owned were a 1948 mercury convertible with a flat head engine, I had problems with the carburetor, so I found a carburetor on a Buick at the junk yard, made an adapters and installed it on my mercury it worked grate and had more power.

In the earlier years all Fords cars had a voltage regulator to regulate the charging of the battery, In later years general motors' had an alternator with built in diodes to keep the battery charged, I would go to the junk yard and find an alternator on a cheverlot, get it and replace the Ford regulator with the alternator and rewire it and have a more reliable charging system.

In the early 1980's about a mile from my house was a race car shop that built Nascar race cars, one of Nascars most popular drivers asked me if I could make him an adapter that would lock the rear-end of his car while he was qualiffng for a race. At that time I had a small shop in the back yard, so I proceeded to design and made a device that could be installed on the rear axel where the inspector could jack up one rear wheel and spin it to make sure the rear end was not locked, and when you let the wheel back down the rear end would automatley lock giving the car more traction with both wheels pulling at the same time and at the same amount, Nascar's rules would not let you run a locked rear-end, this device were used with great success. These types of things were always a challenge and I enjoyed doing this type of work, part of racing back then was to cheat but not get caught.

I also cut and shortened a drive shaft for this same driver, and when he had it picked I told the owner that he had to take it to a place in Charlotte and have it balanced, he said he would but I found out that he did not, the car was taken to a Nascar track in Talladega Alabama and turned a lap at over 200 miles per hour without any vibration, this was before they were required to run restrictor plates. I thought that were amazing.

I was always pearty crazy with a car, in 1963 I had bought a new 1963 1/2 ford fast back, at that time my uncle Mack was still living and we went to visit him every weekend, and I always went new town road from 521 in Indian Land to Monroe and returned the same way, I started checking my watch when I got on new town and would check it again when I reached Monroe, I would try and cut off minutes each trip until I was getting sideways on the curves and the tires screeching around each curve. One time my boss went with me to Pageland, and when we come back it was late at night, and when I got on new town road out of Monroe he never spoke for the whole time until we reached 521 in Indian Land, he just sat and looked ahead, when he did speak he said that was an scary ride.

I was always doing some crazy things back then, if the Lord were not taking care of me I wouldn't be writing this today. I have often wondered why I didn't get killed or killed someone else; I guess God had other plans for me later.

In the early seventies I designed a device that could be mounted under a carburetor with a chamber and heating coils built inside and attached to the exhaust manifold, that would pre heat most any type fuel or oil to the point it would be combustible enough to burn just like gas as it passed through the carburetor. I tested it on a motor, and once the motor was started on gas it could be switched to this fuel and it would perform well, until it were turned off and cooled down, it would then have to be restarted on gas to reheat.

I was always fascinated with solar power, to the point I built a solar boiler consisting of seven large magnifying glasses mounted in a round cylinder with the magnifying lenses adjusted so they would be directed on a round copper plate with coils soldered to the underside, the coils were configured in a way that water could be passed through them at a slow velocity and would turn the water to steam as it passed through the plates and traveled on to the tank, and as it cooled it would condense back to hot water. I also designed a device with an electronic eye that would rotate the face of the magnifying glasses toward the sun as it traveled from sunrise to sunset. These devices are still stored in a room of our shop today. My problem was I could design and build some amazing things but promoting my products were something I could never do. I was always a doer not a promoter.

The company I was working for was making some changes on the spinning frames so a doffer wouldn't have to lower and raise the frame carriage to doff the yarn by hand. It would take the doffer's about five minutes to lower the carriage, and when finished doffing it would have to be raised using a crank. They come up with a hydraulic lift using cylinders to lower and raise the carriage by pushing a button that took only a few seconds. This system had been installed on a group of frames and after a short time they started having problems with the pumps. They had designed the process using a hydraulic pump on each frame. Two of the engineers and I were in the cafeteria eating lunch one day and they were talking about the problems they were having with these small pumps, after thanking about it a few minutes I asked them why they were using a pump on each frame instead of one larger pump for several frames with hydraulic lines going to each frame with a control on the frame, because all the frames would never be doffed at the same time so there were no reason why this wouldn't work. They went back to the chief engineer and told him what I had said and he agreed with the idea. He talked with the legal department about what could be done to get a patent on this operation. A few days later I got a summoned to come to the legal department, when I got there, there were several people in the room and I was told that wanted to apply for a patent on this design and it would have to be in my name because it was my idea. So they proceeded to lay out the patent application for me to sign, I had no problem signing the application, and signed it. After I signed the papers they gave me another paper to sign. This paper stated that I agreed for the company to use this idea free of charge, but if they ever let any other company use this idea I would be paid ½ the rolity and the patent holder would get the other half for doing the patent work. It didn't take me very long to figure out that no company would agree for a competitor to use a patent they owned to be able to compete with them.

In the early 1970's the carding dept was having a problem with the selvage edge of the web leaving the card machine and going into what was called a roven can, the edge would have places that would lose fibers and cause the roving to be uneven, this had been happening like this and causing this problem for as long as anybody could remember. I designed a nozzle out of plastic with 1/16 inch holes in a half circle, the shape of cylinder that the web come from and applied a small amount of air pressure to pass through the holes and cause the edge of the fibers to roll over and make the selvage thick enough the fibers would not drop out. I built a prototype in my shop at home on my off time and asked if I could demonstrate it in the card room on a carding machine. I was given permission and installed it, it worked as I expected and when it was proven the plant manger gave me a contract to make and install this device on all the card machines in the plant. That solved a problem that had been going on for years. I was again asked to sign an application for a patent but after what had happened before with the patent application I had signed, and the release form I had to sign, I declined.

When I left springs and went in my own business, I made and sold this device to several other textile companies; it was called a Selvage Control. I remember getting a call from a textile company in Shelby inquiring about my selvage control and wanted to try one, this was a company that was almost impossible to become a vender for, I went to the plant and installed one and they couldn't believe how good it worked, I also got a call from another plant in Pineville NC and installed the control on seven cards for them, that were about the time textiles were leaving this country and a few years later about all these plants were closed.

When I worked for Springs Mills as an air condition mechanic in the late 1960's we had controls throughout the plant that were pneumatic that controlled the tempeture and humidity. These controls had an element that was sentive to humidity. The only problem was the elements would get lint on them and would not work properly, causing the condition in the room to widely fluctuate. These controls sent an air signal to a valve that controlled water pressure going to the evaporator motor grid inside the duct which would control the amount of humidity the duck would put out. I designed a control consisting of two thermostat probes, one with a cloth sock on it and a tail going into a small container filled with water, the sock would draw water up and keep the probe wet. With this configuration the humidity could be measured and controlled through the same valves that were used with the original controls. This eliminated the fluxration of the temperature and humidity that were caused with the element that were used originally. I got permission from management to install this device and monitored it for several weeks, using recording charts, the results were amazing. A few weeks later I was offered a promotion to supervision at another springs plant, in which I accepted, being so busy on my new job I never had the time to follow up on the control. I still have the handmade prototype control I made for keepsake.

Being on monthly salary and 24 hr call duty I worked for the next eleven years and went in to the plant seven days a week except when on vacation, having employees working on weekends as well as week days and nights I felt like I needed to be there in case they needed me or had questions, To do a job and be good at it you have to be dedicated.

THE AMERICAN DREAM

When I decided to leave the company and go in my own business, I had advanced to plant shop superintendent in charge of all electrical and mechanical equipment, except the machines that actually made the product, throughout the plant and all outside services, with 60+ employees including all shifts under my supervision. When I approached the plant manager on January 1st 1981, who was my direct boss and informed him of my plans, his first words were, I wondered when you were going to do this and asked if I would work one more month for him to get someone lined up for my job, and let him make the announcement, in which I did. In the meantime I already had my shop started and were doing some work that the company used outside venders for, but there were some people in the company through jealousy had complained about me doing work for the company and said it was a conflict of interest when in fact I were saving the company money on the work I did on my time off. A week before the 1st of February in our daily meeting the manger told all in the meeting that he had an announcement to make, and he proceeded to tell everyone that I were leaving the company the first of February and asked them all to help make me successful, and said there would be no conflict of interest any more, I can't explain how good this remark to my peers by the manger made me feel, and I will always be grateful for Springs for providing a job to help raise our family. My wife, two sons and I have always had a special relationship with Springs Mills.

Earlier after we bought our house, we had a septic tank installed for the bath room, it worked well for a few years until the drain stopped working and septic water started coming up in the back yard and created a mess, I didn't have the money to have it dug up and replaced, at that time, so I went to the local hardware and bought three sticks of dynamite and drilled a two inch hole in deferent location with a hand ogar, and placed the dynamite underground by the side of the drain line and used two wires and a flashlight battery to set the dynamite off, it broke up the dirt around the drain line and it worked good for several years. I used this same idea for the two inch well that we had drilled a few years earlier when it quit producing water, the well were about seventy feet deep with about fifty foot of it drilled through blue granite rock, so I tied two full sticks of dynamite together and lowered it to the bottom of the well with a blasting cap attached and two wires coming to the top of the ground I used a battery to set the cap off, when I blasted the bottom of the well it broke up the rock and let water come in through the cracks, I used this well at least ten more years with all the water we needed, until the pump went bad and I had a new six inch well drilled.

About that time I had a friend who had a large oak three in his front yard that had been struck by lighting and died, he had cut the tree down and removed it, but he could not get the stump up, I asked him why didn't he blow it out with dynamite, and he asked me if I would do it for him, I said I would if he would buy the dynamite, a few days later he told me he had the dynamite, That evening after work I went to his house and placed the dynamite all around the stump, more than it really needed, and asked him to move his car which was parked a fairly good distance away, he looked at me and said it won't hit the car that far away. But I insisted he move the car. I rolled out the wire a good distance from the stump and told him to get behind a big tree that were about forty foot away, when I touched the wires to the battery, it sound like a large bump as the ground shuck and the stump come out of the hole, it looked like slow motion as it went about thirty foot in the air and started to fall toward his house. I will never forget the look on his face as the stump was traveling overhead. Thankfully it landed a few feet from his house. Again God had protected me when I was doing stupid things.

Another time I used dynamite was when I was building an underground room at my house, I was using a backhoe to dig it out and kept hitting large rock, so I decided to go and get some dynamite and loosing the rocks up. One evening about 6 pm I placed the dynamite and being at our back kitchen door my wife were cooking supper right inside the door, I didn't think to warn her of what I were going to do, so I set the dynamite off and small rocks with a few larger ones rained down on the roof over the kitchen after they were blown out of the hole. My wife come out the back door asking what was going on. I didn't do that anymore without her getting a warning first.

On this same hole that I were going to build a room in, After I finished the digging out the hole I had to put all the framework in place, one afternoon I come home from work and went to the site and started the frame work, I had left my skill saw out the night before and we had a shower of rain and the saw got wet, Skill saws back then were all metal, and when I started to cut a piece of board I somehow got grounded and couldn't get loose from the saw, it was shocking me so bad I was shaking and trying to get loose, luckily while I was moving around I fell backwards in the hole pulling the saw out of my hand as I fell, I got skinned up but thankfully I got loose from the saw, Again God had saved me form surely being elecuted. From that day on I always made sure I never used a power tool that wasn't completely dry.

Another time I had a close call I was working in the shop at Springs and one of my duties was to clean the lent out of the spinning frame motors, we would use a roller picker device to get lint out of motor windings, this device was an air motor with a round blade mounted like a drill bit would be mounted in a drill chuck, this air motor ran at a very high speed when air was applied, we would always stop the frame off and use the roller picker blade to go in the electric motor and collect lint on the blade while it was spinning, and when you pulled it out you would strip the lint off the blade with your fingers and go to the next one. These electric motors were powered by 600 volts, that's why it was important to stop the frame which cut the power off, well I would get in a hurry and found I could clean the motors without stopping them, and this went on for a sometime with no problems until one day I stuck the blade in a motor that had a piece of insulation missing and when it touched the naked winding it felt like someone had hit me in the head with a sludge hammer and the roller picker went one way and I went the other, luckily the power were so strong it knocked me loose. Nobody had to tell me after that to stop the frame off. I was too embarrassed to ever tell anyone about this until now, but thank God I was ok, and had learned a valuable lesson.

I started doing repair work in a small shop behind our house in 1976 when I had a 20x 30 building built when we had two extra rooms built on our house and I used it for a shop. I managed to get a collection of equipment, mostly used and restored and built other things I needed. I started doing any kind of machine work people wanted me to do, from fixing something for a farmer to doing special work for large business, I would work in my shop when I was off from my regular job, and a Nephew I haired to work in the shop when I was working on my job. I also used my two sons to work after school; the business was called CD Steen and Sons. I still worked at Springs and continued to work there until February 1981, my two sons Rick and Robby went in the business with me, we have been working together until the present. We had some hard times when we first went in business but we worked hard and spent our money wisely and it got better as we went along and today were doing well. We have always believed that anything could be repaired, but you had to do so only if it was cost effective and the durability would be as good or better then a new part, in most cases I found it would be.

A year or so after we went in our business we were asked by a supervisor at Springs if we could repair tapes for the DSL weaving looms. We talked to a friend of ours who knew a person who had repaired them before and said he knew what kind of equipment needed to repair them but it would have to be fabricated. After talking to him about what we needed I knew we could build the jigs and cutters to do the job. So we started building the equipment and started repairing a few to make sure they worked the way they should. We gave the supervisor at the plant several to test, and after adjusting to his recommendations we started repairing them on a small volume.

After they used our repaired tapes for a while, and we continued to improve on the quality the supervisor told us that our tapes worked better and lasted longer than the machine manufactures new tapes. We continued to repair tapes, not only for Springs but for several other textile companies as well, as the word got out about the quality of our work. We continued to repair tapes for several other companies across the Eastern United States until the textiles started leaving this country and going overseas and plants started closing down. The secret to being successful is always work toward being the best at anything you do and settle for nothing less.

After the DSL sutteless looms started to disappear in the textile industry we started repairing shuttles for the newer Sulser looms. They were small and all metal, the ends would get worn or braded up and the grippers inside would get weak. We found a way to weld the tips back and regrind them back to the standard size, polish the body and replace the grippers by reinstalling the rivets and polish them back to new condition using a vibratory we bought, they had to be perfectly slick with no burs or scratches. We had to design and build equipment to test them. To make sure the grippers would hold. You couldn't tell our repaired from new. We repaired these shuttles for several years until the textile industries started leaving this country and going overseas.

We started working on open end feed shafts for the spinning department in textiles. We found they were having problems with the feed shafts slipping and not holding due to bad clutches. These clutches were about two inches in diameter and had a small coil to magnetize and pull them in when engaged. The clutch disk would get worn or the coil would go bad or other parts would need to be replaced. We would make our own coils when needed, these feed shafts had to hold at least 10 inch pound of torque when engaged. We repaired feed shafts for deferent textile companies across the southeast until again the textiles started being made overseas.

We still have all this equipment stored in our shop, there is no other equipment in the world like what we built, because it was special built for the job and we didn't sell it to compedetors. After most textiles were gone in this country we started designing and working with other companies to design equipment they needed for special type manufacturing. It has always been a challenge for us to build something that would help do a job that no tools were available to do.

When we got in the golf cart motor business it happened without us trying to get in this business. It all started when we started playing with a cart we had at the business and started looking for ways to make it faster. As we found ways to get more torque and speed some of our customers started asking questions about how we got that cart to run that fast. We would never tell anybody what we did and, then we got challenged to race a guy with a gas cart, ours was electric, so we raced him and beat him pretty bad and from then on everybody wanted one of our motors.

We decided to take our golf cart to Pageland drag way and see what kind of speed we could get. I told Robby we should set a goal of 80 miles per hour in the 1/8 mile, and he agreed. Our first run was 86 mile per hour, and Robby decided we should raise the goal to 100 miles per hour which is much harder to reach as we found out. We continued to work toward our goal until we achieved it with a world record of 103 miles per hour.

We began to see the business possibilities in upgraded golf cart motors. That is when we started building a few motors for some of our friends and they told there friends and it started growing, and today we build and ship motors across the nation every day. A few years back we decided to attempt a run for the Genius world record for the fastest golf cart, when we contacted Genius world records we were told they didn't have a class for the world record for a golf cart. We asked if they could open a class and they said they would and sent us the rules. This being the first attempt they didn't have a speed for us to beat. After a month or so we were ready to make an attempt and went to a local drag strip and made the run. We ran a little over 90 mph in 1/8th mile and got all our paper work together and sent it in only to get it turned down. When we asked why, they said it had only one seat and a golf cart would carry two people. So we informed them that we would get a golf cart off the golf course and prepaid it for an attempt. They agreed for us to make another run but now we would have to run at least 90 miles per hour because we had proven that a golf cart would run that fast.

We proceeded to get our cart ready along with doing the work we had to do to keep our business going, to pay the bills and feed our families. We worked on the cart and motor for several months getting it ready. We then had to take it to the drag strip and test to make sure it was race ready and safe to run at those high speeds. In order to get a world record you have to have the clocks verified for accuracy by getting a certification from the manufacture of the clocks, and have at least two witnesses to sign that they were at the event and verified the speed, it had to be witnessed and signed by a notary public. We had to have videos to show the attempt run and the score board. We had five go-pro cameras mounted on the golf cart with a full set of clubs on the back. The cart was capable of playing a full round of golf caring two people.

When we went to the track to make the attempt, we started out slow to see how the cart handled and increased the speed as we made several runs, on the last test run we picked up a screw in the right rear tire, and drove back the return road to where we were pitted with a half flat tire. After looking things over we decided to plug the tire and inflate it and make the attempt run, we did and run 103.65 mph in the ¼ mile setting the Guinness World Record for the fastest golf cart.

THE AMERICAN DREAM

One year later we asked Geneses to let us attempt to break our own record and they agreed. We made some changes like going from lead acid batteries to Lithium which dropped our weight approxley 700 pounds. When we made the attempt we run a speed of 118.76 miles per hour in a ¼ mile at Darlington drag way My son Robby who drove the cart said he promised God, if he let him have one more safe run he would park the cart and not run it again. And it hasn't been run again. When he crossed the finish line the front wheels were still lifting off the track with an eighty pound block of lead on the front bumper and the controller set at only 80% throttle. When we sent all of our videos and paper work in to Geneses they checked and processed it and we were notified that we were issued the second world record breaking our old record.

After I left Springs and had been in our business for a few years my sons Rick Robby and myself went to a car show in Charlotte NC and I saw an electric pickup truck a man from Monroe had built, I had always been amazed with anything electric, after looking at the truck and talking to the owner I saw several things that I thought I could do to improve the way it was built and improve the performance of the truck. I asked a lot of questions and the guy was very open to answering my questions and even told me he would sell me parts or tell me where I could buy parts he didn't have, when we come back home I couldn't get that truck off my mind. A few weeks later my other son Rick was talking about trading for a new truck and I saw where I could get me a good truck to make an electric with, I told him not to trade his truck on a new truck, because I wanted it to convert to electric, he looked at me like he thought I was losing my mind but said ok. So he bought a new truck and gave me the old one, it was a 1986 Nissan with over 100000 miles but had been taken good care of and looked like new. I visited the guy in Monroe and ordered an electric motor with all adapters to install it, and a controller, contactor and wires. When I got back home I removed the motor, radiator, and all the components I didn't need and started preparing it for an electric motor. After hours of making battery boxes and hinges to tilt the body to get to the batteries I started installing the parts to convert it, people would walk by and shake their head and I knew what they were thinking but I knew what I was doing. After I got everything ready for the batteries I went to Gastonia NC and bought 20- 6 volt deep cycle Trojan batteries which would be 120 volts when installed in series. I continued to put everything together and started to see that all components worked and drove it out. It had fairly good performance, but I wanted it to perform better. It had a 400 amp controller and I thought what would happen if I bypassed the controller and let all the power go to the motor at once to get the truck moving and then come back on the controlled so you would have control of the speed while driving. When I made the bypass by using an extra contactor and a micro switch under the accelerator paddle, I drove it out and when I mashed the accelerator to the floor it made the micro switch that closed the bypass contactor and the rear tires started spinning, I knew then I had found what I wanted.

In the mid 1990's we were contacted by a large company named Cato's in Charlotte NC and asked if we would work with them on developing a system to travel on a tram rail so their employees could pick up goods and place them in the basket to be shipped out to their stores. After looking at what they wanted to do, we come up with a basket made of high density propylene and designed it where each side would fold down to load the products and could be latched back up. We designed all the dollies to run on the tracks and go around curves, it worked out great and we built several hundred that were used in there destitution center for years with very little maintance.

For the next few years we took our electric truck to several shows and continued to work toward getting better performance and finding ways to improve upon the components we designed, by working on the brakes to eliminate drag and added air pressure to the tires to help roll residence I got the range up to 70 mile on a charge, and from 0 to 60 mph in less than 15 seconds, the total weight of this truck were over 4500 pound. Everywhere I showed it people could not believe the power and range we got, in the early 1990's 70 mile range in an electric vehicle was unheard of. A guy in Raleigh was showing a Ford ranger pickup with a factory conversion and factory backed, and he was bragging about getting 40 mile per charge and said they were starting with dc volts and converting to ac volts. I ask him why they converted to ac and he said it was for range, and when I told him I got seventy miles on a charge and didn't convert to ac, he didn't seem to won't to talk about it anymore. But I had documented proof of what we had done.

After the word got out that we worked on electric vehicles I was contacted by a gentleman in New Jersey asking about converting a Bat Mobile from gas to electric. This was for Six Flags where they had shows where bat man would drive the bat mobile in the arena; the one they used had a 350ci automobile gas engine which always gave troubles with gas fumes and noise. We agreed to build all the electrical components and install them and when we finished they were well pleased, saying it sounded like a turbine which they liked. We ended up building two of the eletric Bat Mobiles.

In the mid 1990's I decided to design an electric drive axle that could drive a direct drive axle and be able to change the speed from 1st gear to 2nd or high gear by using two drive belts one on each side of the axle, with deferent ratios, when one was engaged the other would be disengaged, that could be accomplished with an electric clutch on each side, with one engaged and the other disengaged and vise versa, a friend of mine saw the design and asked I would install one in a porch convertible he had, after working out the details I decided to work with him, I built the drive unit and the battery boxes and one of his mechanics and myself installed it, and when we drove it out the first time, it went 55 mph and changed gear ratios by flipping a switch. The axle were built with a gear setup in such a way the axle could be rotated by the outside housing and the wheels on each end would be independent so you could go around corners without one wheel spinning or dragging, The drive motor was 120 volts dc with a 120 volt battery pack, and 400 amp. Controller, the range was about 70 miles with the batteries weighing approxley 1200 pound plus the weight of the car. We were issued a United States patent on this drive axle.

A year or so later we decided to build an electric drag car using 120 volts. We used lighter 12 volt batteries to conserve weight knowing we didn't need the range, and for drag racing we needed to be as light as possible. We had got an old bumper car that were used at Carowinds theme park, and had been discontinued, we only needed the body, and made our own chassis which was really much too heavy but we used what we had, after building the chassis and installing all components, motor, controller, contactor and batteries I was ready to test it, it was setting between our buildings and headed toward a bulldozer, when I got in and got set, checked the brakes and started to go a short distance to check and see if everything worked ok, when I hit the accelerator it hung wide open and the drag car lunged toward the bulldozer, and the brakes wouldn't hold it back, finely the battery main cable burned into and it stopped, real scurry with it going toward the bulldozer blade. When we got everything fixed and tested we carried it to Mooresville drag strip and done some more testing we were running a disappointed 70 miles per hr in the 1/8th mile, we had a straight drive transmission and the linkage wasn't working the way it should and we could never get gears to change properly, and the chassis was way too heavy to get any performance, we brought it back and continued to work on it, getting the shifter working better and tuning up the electrical components. We never took it back to the drag strip but did get an invitation to drive it in the pace lap at charlotte motor speedway before the world 600 race, which we did and it was a big hit.

From then forward we always were looking for deferent ways to work with more electric projects. The next project was with John Deere and an electric riding lawn mower. They had heard about us and wanted to know if we could build an electric riding mower or modify a gas mower to electric. We looked at their mowers and told the VP of marketing that we could modify their gas to electric and gave them a price if they would furnish us with a new riding mower to use, they agreed and delivered a new Sabra riding gas mower to our shop, in the meantime we had designed that drive axle for an electric vehicle that could be driven by a chain and both wheels would pull but would go around curves without the tires dragging or spinning, we built an axle the right size for the mower and used a notch belt to drive the mower, we used a 36 volt golf cart motor mounted vertical to drive the blades and pull the vehicle it had a reverse through a hydraulic valve that would change the direction of the vehicle, the blades would always run in the same direction. When we finished it would cut 1 acre of grass on a single charge, the batteries were mounted in this order, 2 under the hood and 2 in the back behind the seat and 2 over the rear wheels, with all body work to accommodate the batteries, we measured one acre in a field with grass about 6 inches high and cut it on one charge with power left, we also videotaped the process. When we invited them to come to our shop and look at the finished mower and test it, they come and we presented them with the video, one of the guys asked me if it would cut the grass on the side of a road through a field from our shop, the grass was about two foot tall an thick, I told him to get on it and cut it, he thought it would bog down but to his surprise it cut the tall grass and the motor never slowed down. I found out later that they had been trying to get an electric mower to cut grass for two years at one of their locations but had no success and that guy was one of the engineers working on it. After talking with the chief engineer at John Deere I learned about their work on the mower and he told me that we had exceeded their expectations. He also said that they would never manufacture an electric riding mower unless the consumer demanded it, they only to know the feasibility of it working.

We continued to work on several electric projects and still find them satisfying.

After we finished the mower for John Deere we decided to build one from scratch and design it the way we thought would work better, and we proceed to build it, it took several months to build because we had to do whatever it took to pay the bills first, we made and installed five eight inch blades on our design deck. With shorter blades we could to turn the blades faster which would cut the grass smoother and not exceed the federal regulations of speed at the tip of the blade, When we finished and tested it by cutting over an acre of grass on a charge, and we had also built a trailer that could be pulled behind the mower with an ac inverter mounted under the bed with two twelve volt deep cycle batteries to convert the power to 120 volt ac that would run any 120 ac implements like a string trimmer, blower or even an electric chain saw, everything worked great and we still have it in our shop show room along with other things we designed.

Another thing we designed and was very successful was a chain saw that could be mounted to a string trimmer by replacing the trimmer head with the saw, we used a bar from a 16 inch chain saw and cut it down to seven inches and machined the head adaptor and mounted the blade and chain with the shaft mounting to the threads on the string trimmer, this was long before manufactures come out with this attachment on their trimmers, we could not only reach up and cut limbs off trees but could cut up to six inch diameter trees down, this attachment was simple to change by screwing one attachment off and the other on. We have video tapes of the saw working.

On September 25, 1999 one of worst things happened to me that had ever happened before, I lost my loving wife of over forty years and the mother of our two sons to cancer, I can't even start to explain what we went though and the heartache it caused for all of us, she was the most wonderful wife and mother any one could ever have, almost eighteen years has passed and it's still so hard to write about it today, it still hurts so bad. Even with God giving me another wonderful wife that have helped me through the hard times and I love her very much it still hurts. But through the help of God, my boys, and my present wife which have helped and loved me so much I have learned to live my life without her and try to make my family as happy as possible, and thank God we all get along good.

When we started working on golf carts go back several years before we started working on carts for the public. It started when I had a cart I bought from a friend and used it around the property for a few years when one day I decided to see what I could do to speed it up and get more power. After working with several parts and testing we kept finding ways to help the power, and we started to work on the motor and doing some fine tuning and got more rpm, which is more speed. With our customers coming in and seeing the speed we had got out of this cart they started asking questing and wanting us to get their cart to run faster, from then on we started helping our friends get more speed and torque for climbing hills, and it went from there to drag racing carts that we were very successful with. We had people at the drag strip watch our run and start shaking their head and say; I saw it and still don't believe it. We got a lot of perblisty drag racing golf carts and people started calling, wanting us to work on their motors and our golf cart business started to mushroom from there.

In 2006 Sun City were starting to be built off 521 in Indian Land about eight miles south of our shop. This is a golf cart friendly community with only 55 years and older residents. We started buying golf carts that had come off the golf courses when they were replaced with new ones. We would take these carts, recondition them and add accessories such as back seat kits, mirrors, fancy wheels and our Plum quick motors and any other accessory a customer wanted. We made these carts available to any one that wanted them. When the residents of Sun City found out we built these carts and the quality we built in them, they started coming to our shop and asking us to build a cart for them. As we got several carts in the community the word got around and over the next several years we built and sold over 400 carts for our Sun City customers. We built these carts and had to keep up our motor business as well.

We would also service all the carts we built and do repair work for anybody who bought their cart somewhere else. We always treated our customers with respect and tried to be as honest as we could with them. After I had my heart surgery I had to slow down and finely quit building carts but I will still help my customers any way I can, and make suggestions for them on what they can do and recommend where to get help, where I know they will be treated fairly and be satisfied with the work.

We now ship our modified motors all over the United States and some foreign countries. When our motors started to sell we called them Plum Quick and the name stuck and is now well known all across the country as the best and fastest golf cart motors available anywhere. We later run for and received the Geneses World Record for the fastest golf cart with Robby driving it. The speed was 118.76 miles per hour at Darlington drag way in Hartsville SC, a ¼ mile track. By getting the world record the news media carried it all over the world and our business really picked up and continues to be strong.

We always treat our customers fairly and try to help them any way we can. When you do that they will have faith in your work and tell their friends that you can be trusted, and that goes a long way toward picking up more regular customers that will call you when they need information or a service you have to offer. It's all in being honest.

Two and a half years ago I had triple bypass surgery and thank God I am doing great, I had what I think was one of the best heart surgeon anywhere and a man of faith that done an outstanding job, and with my two Sons and their families and my wife who waited on me hand and foot until I got back on my feet, I thank them with all my heart, without all of them, I don't know what I would have done, I've been blessed to have them, and with all their concerns about me working so much I have slowed down a little, but I still keep busy. I learned a long time ago if you listen to your body and do what it tells you to do, you will know when to hold back and slow down, and always have faith and give God the thanks for taking care of you and put your life in his hands and listen to the doctors that have faith in him to guide and help you, but you must do what they recommend and what you know is right.

I believe I have a lot of knowledge and technical information I can still pass on to others to help them in the future. At present I am working with my two twin grandsons and trying to pass some of my experience to them that could help them in the future, and thankfully they are learning and have a great attitude.

I was blessed with two boys that have become two great young men with children of their own. They both are hard working and in church on Sundays with good wives and both work together in the business we started years ago. All my grand kids are boys with one great granddaughter and they all love and respect each other, what else could you won't? My twin grandsons won't to join the business after they finish school, they are being home schooled by their mother and it shows by their actions, and their respect for everybody. It makes me feel good to know they have respect for their father and uncle and won't to work with them. My other two grandsons are doing good as well the oldest has a good job and family and the other is going to school to become a physical therapist. So I've been blessed.

We continue to make improvements and look for deferent ways to make the performance of our golf cart motors even better. We are working on another cart that we hope to brake our old record, but business have been so good we haven't had the time to work on it lately but hopefully we will get back on it soon, it takes a lot of time doing the development and testing. Our goal is to break the 130 mile per hour mark in a ¼ mile drag way in a golf cart which we know is possible but it takes a lot of work and testing and making sure everything is safe which always comes first.

Over the years I have seen many things take place that when I was a young boy I would never have dreamed some of these things could ever happen in our country, like the President of the United States being assonated November 22nd 1963, a man landing on the moon July 20th 1969, or two air planes being flown into the trade center buildings killing 3000 people September 11th 2001, these things was unthinkable back in the 40's and 50's In the United States of America, plus all the shooting that are happening every day across the country. It makes you wonder what all this will lead to in days to come. It seems more and more people have lost all morels and don't care about anyone but them self, when I was a kid drugs were unheard of, and guns was used only for hunting and used by the military in wars. When you had a disagreement with someone the worst you would do would be get in a fist fight and it would be over when the fight was over, now somebody have to die for them to get satisfaction. One of the problems is what our young people are taught in school and in some homes as well, they see people doing drugs and killing others and think this is the way you supposed to live; thank God we still have some people with the morels to do what's right and have respect for life.

The most amazing thing for me was when a man landed on the moon in 1969, as I listened to the landing on the radio and heard Neal Armstrong say the Eagle has landed and later when he stepped on the surface of the Moon and said, One step for man and one giant leap for mankind, It made the hair stand up on the back of my neck. The bold promise by President John F. Kennedy to put a man on the moon in this decade had been kelp. It was unfortunate he didn't live to see it take place.

Two more of the most sad things for this nation was when the President was assonated November 22nd 1963 by Lee Harvey Oswald and when two planes were flown into the Twin Trade Centers Towers on September 11th 2001 killing close to 3000 people. I watched the 2nd plane fly in to the tower live on TV; it was the most terrible sight I had ever seen. I watched on television as the plane approached the second tower and hit it and exploded leaving a gaping hole. Watching the after math and clean up was the most heart braking and sad moments you could live through, knowing what had happened and knowing we have people in the world that would go to these extremes to kill our people.

It was a sad day for the United States when it was announced that President Kennedy had been assonated on November 22nd 1963, and when they showed reruns on Television would make chills come all over your body, it's an awful thing when the leader of the free world gets assonated. We never know what can happen, and with the World the way it is today we can only pray that these kinds of things never happen again. The President of the United States is our President regardless of party or whether you like or dislike him, he is our President.

On September 21st 1989 Hurricane Hugo hit Charleston South Carolina and continued to move through the state with devastation in its pass. When it reached Fort mill South Carolina it still had hurricane force winds and the damage was hirable, I remember when the wind and rain hit and you could feel the house tremble and after a while everything got calm and the wind stopped for about 15 minutes and all of a sudden it started again from the opposite direction, that was when the eye of the storm was directly over us and when it passed over we got the back side. When it calmed down that time I went outside and saw trees down, roofs off buildings and we had no power for days. I remember trying to get out to check on my children about five miles down the road when I found trees blown down across the roads. I had to return and get a chain saw to cut trees out of the roads, when I finely got the roads passable I continued to check on my two children and their families. Thank God they were ok. But there were debris and trees down everywhere you looked. This was one of the worse storm I had been in.

I guess the worst was a Tornado that I and some of my coworkers were caught in on business twenty one just outside Fort Mill one day around 1:00 P.M... We were coming back from lunch in Charlotte and approaching the town limits, I was in the back seat of the 1969 Oldsmobile which was a heavy car, when I felt the car lift off the highway and set down on the shoulder of the road, we didn't know what had happened, only that the wind had been blowing kindly hard. And when the car lifted and set down, the winds all of a sudden stopped, after setting there a few minutes we continued to pull back on the road and drove a few yards further when we saw trees all over the road, and you could see the path the Tornado had cut through the trees, if we had been 100 yards further down the road we would have been in the center of the Tornado. That was scary.

A few years earlier a Tornado had hit Fort Mill causing a lot of damage. Trees were down and houses had roof damage and some houses completely destroyed. You don't really know how it feels unless you go through these kinds of problems and see the dangers that come with them. I had seen the results of a tornado in 1954, in Jefferson S C when I was fourteen years old, where it destroyed a lot of houses in a streak about a quarter mile wide. It was only about three miles from where I lived at that time. We saw and heard that Tornado as it touched down. You could see full sheets of tin high in the sky where the Tornado had torn it up from buildings. Nature can be a very destructive force.

I remember around 1953 when we had a bad storm come through our part of the country that brought devastation to several homes and barns. Back then the weather forecasters wasn't as accrete as they are today and bad storms was sometimes a surprise when they happened, It started as a thunder storm with the clouds looking yellow and all of a sudden the wind started blowing hard, and I remember it sound like rocks hitting the house and it got so loud you couldn't hear anything but that noise, it only lasted for a couple minutes but it felt like an hour, when it stopped we went outside and found the roof gone off our house and several buildings destroyed, and hail was piled up on the ground so thick you could walk across the yard without your feet touching the ground, and around the chimney base, it were piled up a foot high or more some of these hail stones weighed over 2 pound on a pair of scales, and the size of soft balls or larger. This was the most scurry storm I had ever seen, it felt like everything would be destroyed in the two minutes or so it lasted.

Back then everybody farmed in our area and most all of the land were cleared, that being the case there were not as many trees to break the wind and most all the fields were plowed in the spring. That sandy dirt was very dusty and when we had a lot of wind it made it worse. When the wind started blowing in the spring, we called it the March winds, the dust would be so bad you could only see about a quarter mile and at times not that far. You could taste the dust in the air when you were outside. And this would sometimes last for several days. That's how bad it was.

We had to do whatever we could to get the ground ready to plant and hope we would get a shower of rain to settle the dust. Most people don't realize what it was like growing up in those days. Back then it was a way of life and we knew what to expect from year to year, but that didn't make it any better.

Today farming is very deferent from when we were farming, today farmers have tractors with air conditioned cabs and filters to keep the dust out. It's amazing how for technology has come in the past 70 years. I think as people get more things to occupy their minds as they have today they lose a lot of relationships with their neighbors that were so important in the early days. Maybe we are living too fast and have so many things to worry about that it's hard to remember where we come from.

Today we have so much news, mostly bad, readily available and so many bad things going on in the world that it can get depressing and when you get depressed it's hard to concentrate on the things you should. With all the technology we have today that our children have excess to that keep their minds occupied on some of the bad things they see on television, make me wonder what the future will be like a few years from now as they grow up and become our leaders. Most of the values we had growing up, and the respect we had for others is being lost to a deferent attitude and a deferent way of thinking, most everybody seems to think their way is the best way without any reasoning, it always seems to be the way people think today. If this way of life continues, all I can say is God help us, for the leaders of our nation is going to need his help. I've never been one to paint a gloomy picture but that is the way I see it, if things don't change and if we don't start having more respect for each other and start looking for positive things that will help, and be able to talk about them and reach common grounds for the betterment of everybody. Most of our palliations seem to only think about what will helps them get reelected instead of whats good for the country, and can't reach an agreement with each other on anything, even if they know it would be the right thing to do, if it don't benefit them they don't think it's a good idea.

Around October 25th 2019, I had an experience that most people I talked to found hard to believe. I had no problem believing it because I believe in the powers of God and have no dough about what he can do. This started back when I was very young, about 6 years old, when I asked God to help me get a nail out of my foot and He come to my rescue and the nail fell from my foot with no pain. In October 2019, I had a small stroke in the back of my brain that affected my sight, to the point it I could look at any white surface and it would look like black mud had been put on it in spots all over. I put my faith in God and asked Him to return my sight, in about five days my sight had returned to almost as good as it was before. before this happened I had an eye exam and the doctor told me that I had permanent damage in my brain n and my sight would problely not get any better .when I went for a follow up with the newroglist she asked me how my eyes was, I told her I could see as good as I ever could, she looked surprised and asked if I could read? I told her as good I ever could, and she said I was a very lucky man. "I'm a very lucky man, because I have faith in God".

If you have faith in God, and believe in Him there is nothing impossible.

Printed in the United States
By Bookmasters